Evaluating Bibliographic Instruction

A Handbook

ACRL BIS Research Committee
Subcommittee on Evaluation

Mignon S. Adams
Penfield Library
SUNY at Oswego
Oswego, New York

David Carlson
Clifford Memorial Library
University of Evansville
Evansville, Indiana

Bonnie G. Gratch
Bowling Green State University Libraries
Bowling Green, Ohio

Larry Hardesty
Roy O. West Library
DePauw University
Greencastle, Indiana

David N. King
Houston Academy of Medicine
Texas Medical Center Library
Houston, Texas

John Mark Tucker
Purdue University Library
West Lafayette, Indiana

Richard Hume Werking
Trinity University
San Antonio, Texas

Virginia Tiefel, Chair
Ohio State University Libraries
Columbus, Ohio

Evaluating Bibliographic Instruction
A Handbook

Bibliographic Instruction Section
Association of College and Research Libraries
American Library Association
Chicago, Illinois
1983

Contents

Preface

Because the rapid growth of bibliographic instruction is a comparatively recent phenomenon, many instruction librarians have simply not had the time to evaluate what they are doing; and many lack the specialist knowledge about, or experience in, program evaluation. This handbook has been written by librarians (with one exception) for librarians both to offer an introduction to basic precepts of evaluation and to furnish some direction to move beyond the material covered in the handbook.

The subtitle of *A Handbook* has been chosen because the authors wish to stress that this is not the definitive work in library instruction evaluation. It is an introduction to the topic, intended to give general direction, and especially encouragement, to librarians attempting evaluation in this important area.

The handbook is a collection of chapters on various aspects of evaluation and each reflects the author's approach to the subject and style of writing. There is, then, diversity in the writing; and many who critiqued the manuscript noted some inconsistency in style. But as there was no agreement on a uniform style (e.g., between more formal and informal styles), the decision was made not to attempt a major editing of the manuscript. It is hoped that readers will not be distracted by this, and that, indeed, they might enjoy it. Also, the authors invite comments and suggestions, all of which will be retained and referred to the authors of a revised edition.

In closing, as chair I want to thank the members of the committee responsible for the creation of this handbook. No finer group of professionals—working over long time and distance—could have been found. The contributions of several people beyond the committee proved invaluable. They are Katherine Branch, William Crowe, Evan Farber, Constance Finlay, Elizabeth Frick, Martin Gibson, James Kennedy, Tom Kirk, Maureen Pastine, Linda Phillips, Ronald Powell, Daniel Ream, Anne Roberts, and Nancy Taylor.

Deserving of special thanks are Mignon Adams, who collected the manuscripts and supervised their preparation for printing, and Glenda King, who prepared the artwork for several of the charts and tables.

Virginia Tiefel
The Ohio State University Libraries

Introduction

The evaluation of library instruction programs has been a subject of much discussion during the past two decades. Although there seems to have been an increase in the number of published evaluation studies in recent years, it is difficult to tell whether or not this reflects any significant increase in the use of evaluation by the majority of instruction librarians. Evaluation is often assumed to be a complex, time-consuming process; and for those unfamiliar with the methods and tools, it may seem an intimidating prospect.

In fact, evaluation is what you make of it. The process may indeed take on the aspect of a sophisticated educational research endeavor, if that is what you wish. But it is not always necessary to develop large-scale, complex projects in order to profit from evaluation. The process itself is straightforward, easily described in six basic steps.

Step 1. Describe the purpose of the evaluation.

The first step in any evaluation effort is to make sure that you fully understand the reasons for evaluating. Who wants to know and what you hope to learn from the information you obtain will determine the kinds of information you need to collect and how you can best collect it. Chapter 1, "Evaluation and Its Uses," discusses many of the factors which should be considered, and introduces some of the prominent approaches to systematic evaluation.

Step 2. Describe the program in terms of its goals and objectives.

Once you have a clear idea of why the evaluation is to be undertaken, it is important to develop a description of the program as *it currently exists*. Educational programs tend to evolve, and statements of program goals and objectives may not fully detail current practice. Be sure to look for any implied goals and objectives that might not have been included in a formal statement. Chapter 2, "Evaluating in Terms of Established Objectives," provides an overview of behavioral goals and objectives, and explains a taxonomy of educational objectives.

Step 3.   Determine the criteria to be used for evaluation.

When the program has been described in sufficient detail, and the goals and objectives are clearly identified, evaluation criteria can be determined. If goals and objectives have been written with care, this step is relatively easy. Just decide which goals and objectives should be studied within the context of the purpose of the evaluation, and what standards would indicate success. But be sure to consider outcomes which may not have been anticipated by the goals and objectives, or which may indicate undesirable or counterproductive results of instruction. Chapters 1 and 2 include sections discussing the criteria that might serve as standards.

Step 4   Develop the evaluation procedures and overall design of the study.

After the criteria have been determined, procedures for conducting the evaluation can be developed. If the evaluation is to be a major summative effort, or if you intend to monitor your program on a continuing basis by means of evaluation, you may find it useful to develop an evaluation plan based upon one of the approaches discussed in Chapter 1. An appropriate evaluation design should be selected at this point. Chapter 3 provides an overview of some commonly employed designs. The selection of the design will clarify most of the procedures to be used in the evaluation, which instruments might be adopted, and the kinds of statistical analysis that will be necessary. You may find it helpful at this point to set timetables, determine personnel and training needs, and budget for any costs you anticipate. Chapter 3, "Research Designs Appropriate for Evaluating Bibliographic Instruction," introduces concepts related to experimental designs and describes and illustrates their use.

Step 5.   Develop instruments and collect data.

The fifth step in the evaluation process is to develop the instrument or instruments to be used to implement the study. The keys to success in this step involve pretesting the instrument to eliminate any unforeseen errors, and applying the instrument systematically. Deviations in the way data are collected can irreparably compromise the entire evaluation process and render the data useless. Chapter 4, "Data Gathering Instruments," describes a variety of instruments which may be used to collect information, and offers practical advice on choosing an instrument and/or developing your own tests and questionnaires.

Step 6.   Analyze the data and report the results.
Once the data are collected, they should be interpreted within the context of the criteria established in Step 3. The analysis should point out which criteria were successfully achieved, as well as identify components of the program that need improvement. Chapter 5, "Data Management and Statistical Analysis," presents the core concepts of statistical analysis and describes some of the procedures most useful for the analysis of instructional data. Even if a report to outside clientele is not required, writing up the results will help in interpreting and assessing the evaluation results.

Steps in the Evaluation Process

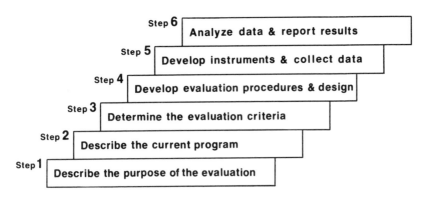

The techniques and methodologies introduced in this handbook may be employed in a number of ways to help understand the effects of your program and improve the quality of instruction. Careful planning and attention to detail are necessary throughout the process.

You will not find the answers to all your evaluation questions here. Each author provides references for further reading, and an annotated bibliography of suggested readings is included. Examples of evaluations and some of the more important sources for information on the evaluation of bibliographic instruction programs are included in Chapter 6, "Significant Works." A glossary is also provided. Even if you follow up on all of the sources mentioned, we encourage you to take advantage of the expertise of others on your campus.

You need not be an expert to succeed at evaluation. Evaluation is not an exact science, and creativity, resourcefulness, and perseverance yield impressive results. Your programs and your students will benefit from the effort.

David King
Houston Academy of Medicine
Texas Medical Center Library

David N. King is Coordinator for User Education at the Texas Medical Center Library Houston Academy of Medicine. He has been involved in all aspects of library instruction for nearly ten years at three different academic institutions.

Chapter One

Evaluation and Its Uses

David N. King

Evaluate!

The rapid proliferation of bibliographic instruction programs in recent years has been accompanied by that admonition. Sooner or later each of us is called upon to make decisions or answer questions concerning our instructional efforts. Evaluation is a means of obtaining the information necessary to make those decisions and answer those questions more effectively.

In fact, instruction librarians evaluate informally as a matter of routine at every stage of educational effort. When presented with the task of orienting new users to the library, we typically attempt to identify their needs, weigh the value of possible topics and facilities for presentation, note the response of the users during the tour to adjust the style or content, and elicit feedback following the orientation. We might then try to decide whether some other approach might be more appropriate. Each time a decision is required in the process, each time an assessment of quality or value is needed, we consider the information at hand and render our best judgment or decision. We evaluate.

Unfortunately, such informal methods are often not sufficient for planning, monitoring, improving, or justifying our educational endeavors. Evaluation, used in its more specific sense, usually refers to a process involving the collection and presentation of information in a manner intended to increase the credibility and usefulness of that information.(1)

Credibility, of course, is a relative term, depending upon the opinion of those for whom the evaluation serves as a source of information. The goal of evaluation is to describe and assess an educational effort and its results in such a way that the information is believable to those who would use it.(2) The value of the information and the success of the evaluation are judged in terms of the usefulness of the results, not in terms of the complexity of the research or the quantity of data generated.

The credibility or believability of information about educational programs is usually determined by the method in which the information is gathered, analyzed, and presented. One way of increasing the credibility of information is to use a systematic approach to evaluation. Although trends are currently moving away from purely quantitative studies, most evaluators and users of evaluation results still believe that the credibility of information depends upon sound objective methods of gathering and interpreting the information.(3) Thus, the major portion of this handbook addresses methods by which information can be obtained and interpreted in a systematic, objective way.

The usefulness of information is obviously dependent upon its credibility, but other significant factors come into play as well. The most important of these concerns **appropriateness;** the information obtained should address the specific information needs of those who would use it.(4) As expert evaluator Robert Stake put it: "There is no comfort in accurate measurement of the irrelevant." The information generated by an evaluation should answer questions that have been posed by you or by others who need to know. You should ask before beginning an evaluation: Who wants to know? What do they want to know? How can the information be obtained.?

A second factor affecting the usefulness of the information is its **practicality:** the information obtained should be meaningfully applicable to the program. It should enable the recipient of the information to judge the effects of the program accurately or make decisions about how the program might be improved. Before you begin to evaluate, you should determine: How will the information be used? What criteria or standards will serve as a basis for judgments and decisions about the program?(5)

It is unfortunate that librarians so frequently equate evaluation with complex studies. Evaluation *can* be a difficult and time consuming process. But in many cases, you need not resort to elaborate research designs or lengthy statistical analysis. In fact, much of the information needed for decision-making by any recipient can be obtained through relatively simple methods. Let the information needs of those who would use the information, not some preconceived notion about educational research, guide you in planning for ways to obtain and deliver that information. If you gather the information systematically, if it is credible and useful for making decisions and judgments about your program, then you are evaluating.

Who Wants to Know?

Evaluations always have an audience (Table 1). In bibliographic instruction, the most common audience, of course, consists of the instruction librarians themselves. But the roles these librarians play in the program may vary, and as a consequence, the kinds of information they expect from an evaluation might differ. Whether the librarian is involved in coordinating the day-to-day instructional activities, administering the program within the organization at large, planning content and developing materials, or teaching, the role will determine the sort of information desired and the level of investigation necessary to yield credible results.

Another audience consists of administrators within the library or the institution who judge the value of your programs and make the decisions about them. The kinds of information they find useful may differ considerably from that sought by librarians directly involved in the program.

Departmental teaching faculty also constitute a typical audience. Their decisions concerning the value of your program for their students may rest upon the evidence you can provide about the significance and strength of your endeavors.

Students and others who would benefit from your program may be influenced in their decision to take a bibliographic instruction course, attend a tour or lecture, or participate in term paper counseling by the presentation of information in a manner credible to them.

Finally, other librarians, especially instruction librarians at other institutions, are always interested in the results of evaluations which may help them plan or improve their own programs.

You will have to decide before beginning an evaluation who the principal audience is. You may discover that several audiences are interested in the same sort of information, in which case the results can be presented in forms appropriate to each. But the initial design of the evaluation study and the most significant presentation of findings should be shaped by the information requirements of your principal audience. The methods which will give the evaluative information greatest credibility to the principal audience should be employed.

Table 1 - Who Wants to Know and What?

Who Wants to Know?	Typical Questions
Administrators	Does the program fit in with institutional goals? Does it have the support of students and faculty? How important are its objectives? Does it fit in with other institutional programs? How does it compare with programs at other institutions? What are the qualifications of those involved? Is the program operating smoothly in terms of time, cost and resources? Is the program educationally sound?
Teaching Faculty	What good is this program educationally? Is it of any value to my students? Does it have the support of other faculty and students? Does it have the support of institutional administrators? What are the qualifications of those involved? Does program content coincide with my course objectives?
Students	Is this program worth my attention? What do I have to lose or gain from it? Is it interesting? Are the teachers any good? How does it fit in with my curricular requirements? Do other students find it interesting and/or useful? Do faculty recommend it?
Program Librarians	Is the program accomplishing what it is supposed to? Are students implementing what they learn? Do we have enough personnel, funding, and support? How much is our program growing or shrinking and why? Is the program having any adverse effects? Is the program running smoothly? Are we doing all we could be or should be doing? How can we improve our program?
Other Librarians	How does that program compare with ours? Is there something in the program that can help ours? Is there anything different or significant about it? Is the program run as it should be? Is the program accomplishing what it is supposed to?

Why Do You Want to Know?

There are several reasons why an evaluation might be undertaken. Whether you wish to evaluate your program for your own purposes, or whether the evaluation is to serve the information needs of others, the intended use of the results is critical in determining what information a study should reveal and what methods might be used. There are three major purposes for evaluating. Evaluation may be pursued for **research**.(6) Studies of this sort attempt, through various strategies, to obtain results which can be generalized to any similar programs. If you could establish, for example, that a particular teaching method is always successful in achieving specific desirable results, that information would constitute generalizable research. Such studies are extremely difficult to conduct in field settings like libraries, where so many environmental, social, and educational factors cannot be controlled. Moreover, research studies are often directed toward collecting information as a means of proving an hypothesis, rather than providing information as a means of improving a program. Nonetheless, some evaluators like Suchman, contend that evaluations of this sort are likely to yield long term benefits to a discipline as a whole.(7)

Evaluation may also be used for purposes of **accountability**.(8) It is sometimes necessary to justify or explain programs to administrators and other educators, especially when funding, personnel, and administrative support are at issue. Library instruction involves a substantial investment in time, expertise, and materials by a library. You may be called upon to justify the expense of your program in times of financial stress, or you may wish to obtain support for expanding your educational efforts. As well as serving as an intelligent response to controversy and administrative pressure, a well-done evaluation can focus attention on a bibliographic instruction program by documenting its progress and accomplishments. Occasions for systematically explaining our programs to faculty, administrators, and students are prevalent, and the value of evaluation as a means of obtaining and retaining support should not be underestimated.(9)

By far, the most fruitful use of evaluation is to accumulate information for educational **decision-making**.(10) All of us are constantly involved in a quest to improve the quality of our programs, and information illuminating the achievements and deficiencies of our instructional efforts may be crucial in assuring successful change. The decisions we make daily about the educational aspects of our programs - whether to change the content of a presentation, whether to to revise the examples in a handout, etc. - are compounded by the

managerial decisions we must make. Unwise decisions concerning the alloca-
tion of educational resources may compromise the quality of other programs,
and could adversely affect library services as a whole. Such decisions are
usually the result of insufficient or inaccurate information. They might be
avoided if we evaluate.

What Do You Want to Know About?

Having considered who wants to know and why, let's take a look at what
can be evaluated.

Evaluators use the term "program" generically to refer to a program in
total or any aspect of that program. When you consider what to evaluate in
your program, the following are likely objects of study:

Instructional Methods.   The value of different teaching methods may be
assessed comparatively, as in a study of the success of a programmed instruction module compared to classroom lectures, or individually, as in the assessment of the results of a course-related instruction session.

Educational materials.   The value of instructional materials, such as handouts, videotapes, and texts, can be assessed either in terms of basic criteria
related to their purpose, or by comparing them with similar items from other
sources.

Students and faculty.   We can gather information about learning, behavior,
and opinion of students and faculty in order to design, implement, alter, or
judge programs. Such information can also be obtained as a means of evaluating
other educational phenomena, such as the effectiveness of an instructional
method.

Teachers.   Information relating to teaching effectiveness can be used to identify the need for more training, or to provide evidence for job evaluations and
promotion and tenure. The attributes and success of teaching librarians can
also be assessed to assist in program management.

Programs.   The achievements and weaknesses of a program as a whole
can be evaluated, either as a means of determining the performance of the
program in accomplishing specific educational ends, or as a way of comparing similar programs.

Usually, when librarians evaluate, they attempt to determine the effectiveness
of their educational efforts. **Effectiveness** is a measure of whether our methods
produce the changes we desire.(11) When we evaluate the effectiveness of our
programs, we try to find out how well our educational efforts are achieving
the intended results.

Although the preceding discussions have concentrated upon the differences between potential audiences and what they might want to know, most educators, administrators, and librarians are interested in knowing whether or not the goals of instructional programs are being met. They want to know what the impact or **outcomes** of the programs really are. In bibliographic instruction, the outcomes of instruction would be measures of behavioral and attitudinal change which can be directly attributed to program efforts.(12)

Unfortunately, outcomes are often difficult to assess. It is frequently necessary to assess instead the intermediate effects of instruction, or program **outputs,**(13) upon the assumption that these findings reflect achievement of program outcomes. Thus, we might try to determine to what extent students learned the information presented in lecture, with the assumption that their new-found knowledge will affect their behavior.

The problem with evaluating outputs rather than outcomes is that there is really no way to assure that the outputs reflect outcomes. For example, the goals of library user education programs usually aim toward an improvement in students' library-use behavior (outcome). The completion of a workbook or passing a test represent the achievement of a certain level of knowledge (output). But knowledge may or may not effect behavioral change - it is necessary but not sufficient.(14)

In addition to accumulating evidence concerning the effectiveness of our programs by evaluating outputs and outcomes, we can also gather information related to program efficiency. **Efficiency** is an assessment of how much effort, time, resources, and money you are investing in a program.(15) Having such information, it is easier to judge whether the program is worth the investment, whether a different approach might be just as beneficial at less expense, or what aspects of a program might be better managed.

How Will the Information Be Used?

When evaluation is employed for decision-making, it often becomes an integral part of the program and serves as a consistent source of information for monitoring and improving educational endeavors. Students and faculty are questioned about their perception of the value of instruction, teaching librarians are asked to comment on classroom proceedings, student performance and learning may be measured, the types and quality of materials are assessed, the procedures for scheduling classes and promoting the program are evaluated, the costs in time and resources are monitored — all with the objective of documenting and improving the program. Michael Scriven, in his seminal work on the methods of evaluation, refers to this as the *formative* role of evaluation.(16) Formative evaluation often involves the use of small studies, like questionaires and tests, at all stages of program development, assuring that a program is progressing as it should. For programs that are evolving due to attempts to improve them or due to forces requiring change, formative evaluation provides guidance for informed decision-making.

On the other hand, evaluation may be used for assessing the quality of a program once it has attained a relatively final form. Scriven refers to this as the *summative* role of evaluation.(17) Summative evaluation usually calls for a single comprehensive study of the entire program, sometimes with the intention of deciding whether the program should be maintained or terminated. Such studies are often comparative, providing information concerning the value of competing programs. For example, you might be faced with a decision between the use of a guided tour or a slide/tape program for orientation purposes. An exploration of the advantages and disadvantages of each, upon which basis a selection could be made, would constitute a summative evaluation. Similarly, an effort to gather every shred of evidence to save a program from the effects of proposed cutbacks due to fiscal exigency or political maneuvering, would constitute a summative evaluation.

What Criteria Will Serve As Standards?

Values play a necessary and inescapable role in the evaluation process, and serve as standards by which the effectiveness and efficiency of a program may be assessed.(18) The nature and sources of these values should be identified during the initial stages of planning for evaluation.

One way of conceptualizing the kinds of values with which evaluation deals is to think of them in terms of benefits. In this sense, values are an expression of being good for something or someone. A bibliographic instruction program is intended to be of some benefit to those attending and to the library, or it would not be undertaken.

Many of the benefits that a program hopes to produce are **explicit,** stated as the rationale for the program, as in a statement of goals and objectives. Other benefits may not be documented or voiced, but are "understood"; they are **implicit** in the purpose and design of the program. These intended results of instruction, whether implicit or explicit, function as a principal source of criteria by which the strengths and deficiencies of a program may be evaluated.

What are the sources of values in library instruction programs? How can you identify the implicit as well as the explicit intended results? The consumer of the educational product is one source: students can be asked what they think the benefits of a program should be, and academic teaching faculty can describe what they think ought to be a positive result or justify purpose of instruction in library skills. Library administrators and those who make decisions about the instruction program may have other criteria by which they judge success. Library users and potential users can reveal what they would consider of value to know about the library and its resources. Finally, librarians (especially instruction librarians) usually have definite ideas about program content, design, and purpose.

As might be imagined, identifying the intended results of instruction is a crucial step in planning for evaluation. The implicit values are equally important as the explicitly stated ones as criteria by which program performance may be evaluated. But not all of the results of instruction can be anticipated, and there is often more to evaluation than simply looking at how well a program achieves its intended objectives. Certainly, many of the beneficial qualities of a program can be found it its intended results. But there may also be **unintended** results.(19)

As an example, instruction librarians might not foresee the full impact of increased use of reference materials as a consequence of their program. Such an occurrence might be seen as beneficial, since it indicates that students learned about the sources presented and are using their new knowledge. However, the occurrence may be considered detrimental by reference librarians, administrators, and other library users if it adversely affects the availability of reference materials and the quality of reference service.

In the effort to establish criteria by which performance can be judged, the intended results, whether explicitly stated or implicit in program design and content, serve as the standards. If program goals and objectives have been carefully written, the task of identifying the positive results of instruction is much easier. It is more difficult to plan for ways of revealing unintended results. Some of the approaches to evaluation discussed below were developed with that objective in mind.

How Do You Judge Program Performance?

The actual effects of instruction, whether anticipated or unintended, are the phenomena that educators normally consider when evaluating. The changes that occur as a result of instruction are the products which indicate the usefulness of a program. Decisions concerning the value, positive or negative, of these effects are referred to as "judgments of worth."(20) Examples of judgments of worth in user eduation include: how well student learning coincides with program objectives, the degree to which instruction improves library-use behavior, and the extent to which attitudes about the library are changed as a result of the program.

Judgments of worth may be distinguished from "judgments of merit."(21) The merit of a program refers to its intrinsic qualities: those values which are inherent in the educational process. The aspects of a program which may be judged on merit include: the training and experience of the teaching librarians, the clarity of the instructional design, or the scope of the program.

Judgments of worth are usually made on the basis of information generated by studies of learning, behavior, and attitudes - the actual effects of the program - in relation to the implicit and explicit goals of instruction and educational values. Judgments of merit, on the other hand, are usually made on the basis of normative criteria or comparative standards which are presumed to indicate quality. Although we tend to think of such standards as being formulated by an accrediting association or institution, just about any judgments based upon the value of what goes into a program, as opposed to the effects of the program, can be thought of as merit judgments. These standards might take the form of a consensus of opinion, such as faculty opinion of the educational background needed by librarians teaching science students, or the standards might be derived by identifying the common elements of programs in libraries in similar settings for comparison.

Most educational evaluation studies concentrate on judgments of worth, and these are probably the sorts of evaluative judgments you will want to make about your bibliographic instruction program. But merit values may serve an important purpose in supplementing or strengthening evaluations. Especially for those outside the program, library administrators, academic teaching faculty, and other librarians, information related to merit may be just as crucial in judgments about your program as information related to worth.

How Do You Plan Your Evaluation?

Evaluation is a relatively new and diversified discipline, and there is no "best" approach to assessing an educational program. Various methods and instruments for collecting and analyzing information are discussed in other chapters of this handbook. But it is often difficult to decide which instruments and methods to use, and when they might be employed most effectively.

Most expert evaluators try to devise a systematic approach to the use of instruments in order to obtain information about a program. The stage during which you collect information and the instrument you employ at each stage determine the credibility and usefulness of the findings. For example, you can use testing as a means of setting objectives in the early stages of a program, or as a means of determining student learning at a later stage. Opinion surveys can be used to establish instructional need, to assess satisfaction with a program during the developmental stages, or after the program is completed as a means of assessing outcomes.

Some of the prominent approaches to systematic evaluation are presented in Table 2. Each approach is intended to provide guidelines for planning, implementing, and using evaluation methods as a means of improving educational programs. As might be deduced from the fact that there are so many different approaches to systematic evaluation, some controversy exists among the experts on what evaluation should do and how best to go about it. A discussion of each of the approaches will not be attempted here, but it might be helpful to consider the types of systematic evaluation and some of their attributes.

Stufflebeam and Webster have grouped approaches to evaluation on the basis of their values-orientation.(22) Evaluation which emphasizes the collection of output information, without concern for whether or not the outputs actually lead to desired outcomes, are referred to as "quasi-evaluation." Approaches which fall into this category include Tyler's objective-based approach, the discrepancy evaluation approach of Provus, and any of the forms of evaluation research. Quasi-evaluation approaches are typically useful for the assessment of student learning, though most of the information accumulated is summative in nature. They have limited value for improving programs, and rarely reveal any unintended results. Nonetheless, quasi-evaluation approaches are often easier to design and carry through, and since they rely so heavily on the familiar process of testing, the use of these approaches is common.

More thorough approaches to evaluation attempt to reveal not only the extent to which pre-established goals and objectives are achieved, but also the outcomes of the program, including any unintended results. Stufflebeam and Webster refer to approaches with this broader values-orientation with the unfortunate term "true evaluation." True evaluation approaches often use many of the same techniques and instruments as are used in quasi-evaluation approaches, but additional methods and tools are employed as well. Approaches which fall into this category include Stake's responsive evaluation, the goal-free approach of Scriven, decision-oriented and naturalistic approaches, Parlett's illuminative evaluation, and the adversary approach.

Many of the approaches appearing in Table 2 require special expertise, and are designed more for the expert evaluator who is called in to study an

Table 2 - Approaches to Evaluation

Method	Emphasis	Application	Strengths	Weaknesses	Proponents
Objectives-Based Evaluation	Assessment of Student attainment of pre-established goals and objectives	primarily summative	Relatively easy to understand & apply	Does not reveal unintended outcomes; Tendency to over-simplify by measuring only what is easily measurable; Concentrates on program content, without means for determining the *value* of the content.	Tyler (30)
Discrepancy Evaluation	Assessment on the basis of performance standards for educational decisionmaking	formative and summative	Provides constant feedback on program progress; Expands and improves on objectives-based methods.	Does not reveal unintended outcomes; Lengthy process requiring time and expertise	Provus (31)
Response Evaluation	Description of program processes and outcomes according to values of key people	formative and summative	Reveals unintended as well as intended results; Comprehensiveness of findings	Requires expertise in variety of formal methods; May be a lengthy and involved process	Stake (32)
Decision-Oriented Evaluation	Collection and analysis of information for decisionmaking	formative and summative	Reveals unintended as well as intended results; Comprehensiveness of findings	May concentrate too much on the value perspectives of decisionmakers; Not all activities are clearly evaluative	Stufflebeam (33) Cronbach (35)
Goal-Free Evaluation	Collection and analysis of information related to actual results rather than pre-established objectives	formative summative	Reveals unintended as well as intended results; Reveals the value of the program as a whole	Requires expert evaluator of high credibility with a variety of skills	Scriven (35)

Method	Emphasis	Application	Strengths	Weaknesses	Proponents
Adversary Evaluation	Evaluation should present two competing interpretations of a program's value	primarily summative	Pros and cons of a program discussed in strongest manner	Requires more people with sufficient skills in both evaluation and presentation; May be too subjective; Not all arguments may be based on true judgment	Levine (36) Owens (37)
Illuminative Evaluation	To illuminate the acceptability of program processes and content	primarily formative	Relatively easy to implement	Kinds of information obtained may not address needs of all audiences; May be open to bias; May be too subjective for many audiences	Parlett (38)
Evaluation Research	Assessment of educational effects for validity, reliability and generalizability	summative	Objectively demonstrated effects	Requires strict controls; Only one or two effects can be evaluated at a time; Little information provided for program improvement	Cooley (39) Suchman (40)
Naturalistic Evaluation	Use of case study, anthropological and sociological methods to comprehensively describe program processes and results	formative summative	Full expertise and sensitivities of evaluator employed; Comprehensiveness of results	usually requires an expert evaluator from outside the program; Highly subjective results which may not be acceptable to all audiences	Guba (41)
Professional Judgment	Assess program on basis of normative and comparative standards	formative summative	Assures that minimum standards are met or that program has value comparable to similar programs	Consists almost entirely of judgments of merit; Little attention to program performance or outcomes	Accrediting Boards and Professional Societies

unfamiliar program, than for the developers and teachers wishing to conduct their own evaluations. Even so, valuable insights into the evaluation process, alternative methods and instruments, interpretation of results, and ways of avoiding common problems, are prevalent in discussions of the approaches.

Major works by the principal proponents of each approach are cited in the table, and the emphasis, strengths, and weaknesses are noted. Since the works of these evaluators are often lengthy, you might prefer to read the overviews of evaluation approaches provided by Popham(23), Gardner(24), Alkin(25), Stake(26), Worthen and Sanders(27), Schulberg and Baker(28), and Stufflebeam and Webster(29).

Conclusion

This chapter has attempted to lay a foundation for evaluation by describing some of the uses for evaluation and discussing some of the elements that go into planning an evaluation. Several of the more prominent approaches to systematic evaluation are also introduced.

The intended results of your instructional effort serve as the basis for establishing evaluation criteria. A well-written, up-to-date statement of goals and objectives is the best source of intended results, and the next chapter provides an overview of how to write and use them most effectively.

It should be reiterated that there is no "best" way to evaluate your program. The instruments and methodologies presented in this handbook should be adopted selectively and adapted to your program to meet your specific information needs. Creativity in the way you look at your program, and systematic planning of the evaluation process, will enable you to profit from the effort.

Suggested Reading

See Bibliography for full entry.

Alkin and Fitz-Gibbon (1975)
Caro (1977)
Cranton (1978)
Gardner (1977)
Morris (1978)
Payne (1974)
Popham (1975)
Provus (1971)
Tyler (1967)
Worthen (1973)

Notes

1. Ernest R. House, *The Logic of Evaluative Argument*(Los Angeles: Center for the Study of Evaluation, UCLA, 1977); and Edward F. Kelley, "Evaluation as Persuasion: A Practical Argument," *Educational Evaluation and Policy Analysis,* Sept.-Oct. 1980, pp.35-38.

2. Methods of presenting information to increase credibility can be found in Lynn Lyons Morris and Carol Taylor Fitz-Gibbon, *How to Present an Evaluation Report* (Los Angeles: Center for the Study of Evaluation, UCLA, 1978).

3. The effective use of qualitative methods is discussed in a number of papers in Thomas D. Cook and Charles S. Reichardt, eds., *Qualitative and Quantitative Methods in Evaluation Research* (Beverly Hills: Sage, 1979); see also Barton B. Proger, "Some Heresy about Linking Routine Decision-Making, Planning, and Evaluation," *Educational Technology,* April 1982, pp. 15-19.

4. This serves as the foundation for decision-oriented approaches to evaluation, such as that of Stufflebeam discussed below.

5. Methods of establishing criteria are discussed by Malcolm N. Provus, *Discrepancy Evaluation for Educational Program Improvement and Assessment* (Berkeley:McCutchan, 1971); and by Carol H. Weiss, *Evaluation Research* (Englewood Cliffs, NJ: Prentice-Hall, 1972); and others.

6. See, for example, Edward R. Suchman, "Evaluating Educational Programs," rpt. in *Readings in Evaluation Research,* ed. Francis G. Caro, 2nd ed. (New York: Russell Sage, 1977), pp. 48-53.

7. Ibid.

8. Many of the decision-oriented approaches stress the accountability issue as an important role for evaluation, for which see references to Stufflebeam's works below. Also relevant are Lois-Ellin Datta, "Does It Work When It Has Been Tried? And Half Full or Half Empty?" *Journal of Career Education* 2, No. 3 (1976), 35-55; and Paul L. Dressel, "Accountability and Attainment of Social Goals," in *Handbook of Academic Evaluation* (San Francisco: Jossey-Bass, 1976), pp. 73-109.

9. See, for example, Larry Hardesty, et al., "Evaluating Library Use Instruction," *College and Research Libraries,* 40 (1979), 309-317.

10. See especially the works of Stufflebeam cited below. Good introductions include Daniel L. Stufflebeam, "Evaluation as Enlightenment for Decision-Making, in *Educational Evaluation: Theory and Practice,* ed. Blaine R. Worthen and James R. Sanders (Worthington, Ohio: Charles A. Jones, 1973), pp. 143-148; and Lee R. Cronbach, "Course Improvement Through Evaluation," *Teachers College Record,* 64 (1963), 672-683.

11. Various interpretations of effectiveness assessment are discussed in Rosemary Ruhig Du Mont and Paul F. Du Mont, "Measuring Library Effectiveness: A Review and an Assessment," *Advances in Librarianship,* 9 (1979), 103-141; for the interpretation used here, see Mark B. Dignan and Patricia A. Carr, *Introduction to Program Planning* (Philadelphia: Lea & Febinger, 1981), p. 108.

12. Charles R. McClure, "The Planning Process: Strategies for Action," *College and Research Libraries,* 38 (1978), 456-466.

13. Ibid.

14. Thus, the advice of most evaluators is to avoid the use of testing as the sole method of program assessment.

15. Dignan and Carr.

16. Michael Scriven, "The Methodology of Evaluation," in *Perspectives of Curriculum Evaluation,* ed. Ralph W. Tyler (Chicago: Rand-McNally, 1967), pp. 39-83.

17. Ibid.

18. See especially Nick L. Smith, "Sources of Values Influencing Educational Evaluation," *Studies in Educational Evaluation,* 6 (1980), 101-118; and David R. Krathwohl, "The Myth of Value-Free Evaluation," *Educational Evaluation and Policy Analysis,* 2, No. 1 (1980), 37-45.

19. See Scriven, cited above. Some of the problems with evaluating in terms of goals and objectives are discussed by Irwin Deutscher, "Toward Avoiding the Goal Trap in Evaluation Research," in *Readings in Evaluation Research,* ed. Francis G. Caro, 2nd ed. (New York: Russell Sage, 1977), pp. 221-238.

20. Egon G. Guba and Yvonna S. Lincoln, *Effective Evaluation* (San Francisco: Jossey-Bass, 1981), pp. 39-52.

21. Ibid.

22. Daniel F. Stufflebeam and William J. Webster, "An Analysis of Alternative Approaches to Evaluation," *Educational Evaluation and Policy Analysis,* May-June 1980, pp. 5-20.

23. W. James Popham, *Educational Evaluation* (Englewood Cliffs, NJ: Prentice-Hall, 1975), Chapter 2.

24. Don Gardner, "Five Evaluation Frameworks," *Journal of Higher Education,* 48 (1977), 571-593.

25. Marvin C. Alkin, "Evaluation Theory Development," *Evaluation Comment,* 2 (1969), 2-7; and Marvin C. Alkin and Carol T. Fitz-Gibbon, "Methods and Theories of Evaluating Programs," *Journal of Research and Development in Education,* 8, No. 3 (1975), 2-15.

26. Robert E. Stake, "The Methods of Evaluating," in *Evaluating Educational Programmes: The Need and the Response* (Paris: OECD CERI, 1976), pp. 18-30.
27. Blaine R. Worthen and James R. Sanders, *Educational Evaluation: Theory and Practice* (Worthington, OH: Charles A. Jones, 1973).
28. Herbert C. Schulberg and Frank Baker, "Program Evaluation Models and the Implementation of Research Findings," *American Journal of Public Health,* 58 (1968), 1248-1255.
29. Daniel L. Stufflebeam and William J. Webster, "An Analysis of Alternative Approaches to Evaluation," *Educational Evaluation and Policy Analysis,* May-June 1980, pp. 5-20.
30. Ralph W. Tyler, "General Statement on Evaluation," *Journal of Educational Research,* 35 (1942), 492-501.
31. Malcolm N. Provus, *Discrepancy Evaluation for Educational Program Improvement and Assessment* (Berkeley, Calif.: McCutchan, 1971).
32. Robert E. Stake, "The Countenance of Educational Evaluation," *Teachers College Record,* 68 (1967), 523-540; and Robert E. Stake, et al., *Evaluating Educational Programmes: The Need and the Response* (Paris: OECD CERI, 1976).
33. Phi Delta Kappa National Study Committee on Evaluation, *Educational Evaluation and Decision Making* (Itasca, IL: F. E. Peacock, 1971).
34. Lee J. Cronbach, "Course Improvement Through Evaluation," *Teachers College Record,* 64 (1963), 672-683.
35. Michael Scriven, "The Methodology of Evaluation," in *Perspectives of Curriculum Evaluation,* ed. Robert W. Tyler (Chicago: Rand-McNally, 1967), pp. 39-83.
36. M. Levine, "Scientific Method and the Adversary Model: Some Preliminary Suggestions," *Evaluation Comment,* 4, No. 2 (1973), 1-3.
37. T. R. Owens, "Educational Evaluation by Adversary Proceedings," in *School Evaluation: The Politics and Process,* ed. Ernest R. House (Berkeley, CA: McCutchan, 1971).
38. Malcolm Parlett and Gary Deardon, eds., *Introduction to Illuminative Evaluation* (Pacific Soundings, 1977); and Malcolm Parlett and David Hamilton, "Evaluation as Illumination: A New Approach to the Study of Innovatory Programs," *Evaluation Studies Review Annual,* 1 (1976), 140-157. For an application to bibliographic instruction, see Colin Harris, "Illuminative Evaluation of User Education Programmes," *Aslib Proceedings,* 29 (1977), 348-362.
39. W. Cooley and P. R. Lohnes, *Evaluation Research in Education* (New York: Irvington, 1976).
40. Edward A. Suchman, "Evaluating Educational Programs," *Urban Review,* February 1969, pp. 15-17.
41. Egon G. Guba and Yvonna S. Lincoln, *Effective Evaluation* (San Francisco: Jossey-Bass, 1981).

Virginia Tiefel is Director of Library User Education at Ohio State University, Columbus, where she has been developing a comprehensive library user education program for the past six years.

Chapter Two

Evaluating in Terms of Established Goals and Objectives

Virginia Tiefel

Introduction

Chapter One discussed important factors to be considered in planning an evaluation. It stressed the importance of identifying those who want the information and why, and what they want to know. Program planners should insure that the information being sought is meaningful and they should have a clear understanding of how the information will be applied in making judgements and decisions about the program. Especially in establishing goals and objectives these important principles must be kept in mind.

Evaluation is an integral part of the process of planning and implementing a library instruction program, but it has been observed that librarians tend to evaluate what they think users need to know rather than give enough attention to determining what users really need. For example, librarians may evaluate students' ability to apply catalog filing rules when what they need to learn is how the use of the card catalog fits into their search for information. Nancy Fjallbrant and Malcolm Stevenson, two writers in the field of bibliographic instruction, urge librarians to gain some sense of identification with users and establish goals and objectives consistent with users' real needs.

Integrating the concept of evaluation into the development of goals and objectives for an instructional program will also help librarians to focus on their aims. This chapter gives special emphasis to evaluation in terms of program goals and objectives, defines and reviews key concepts, and explains how they may be applied in library instruction. Special note is taken of the *B. I. Handbook,* which provides an excellent outline for writing goals and objectives; and numerous examples, which will be examined later, are taken from this handbook.(1) A brief discussion and examples of the application of Bloom's taxonomy of educational objectives provide both background and stimulus for considering goals and objectives in broad educational terms. Some evaluation examples are provided, along with comments on a few essentials about evaluating in terms of goals and objectives. One very important thing to remember in all the steps of evaluation is to utilize the expert knowledge available within the institution. Whatever the need, there is almost certainly someone available for advice and consultation.

Although this chapter focuses on evaluating in terms of goals and objectives, a note of caution should be offered about what some scholars view as pitfalls in the construction of evaluation frameworks in terms of program goals and objectives. They consider strict adherence to predefined goals and objectives as a possible obstruction to an examination of the true results of an evaluation. Indeed, one scholar, Michael Scriven, stresses that goals are important in planning and developing a program, but not in evaluating it. He offers goal-free evaluation as the more valuable method because it focuses on the "actual" effects, not only on those "intended." Actual effects are also referred to as "side" effects, and many consider attention paid to them to be more important or valuable than that given to intended effects. In brief, Scriven believes goal-free evaluation is better because it measures actual effects on demonstrated needs.(2) One must also keep in mind that effects can be so numerous that it is likely to be impossible to predict where they will be found.

Needs

Whether evaluation is goal-free or incorporates established goals and objectives, one must first determine whether there is, in fact, a need for bibliographic instruction. How does one decide this? J. Thomas Vogel suggests that library instruction evaluation begins with three questions:

1. Can library instruction meet student needs?
2. Does it embrace realistic objectives?
3. Is it cost effective?

He states that before objectives can be formulated one must answer the following: who are the users? what are their needs? and how do the users perceive the library and librarians?(3) In this vein, John Lubans surveyed both users and non-users to ascertain whether there was a need for library instruction. He cited a number of studies which conclude that college-level students do not usually have necessary library knowledge, and that therefore instruction is needed.(4)

An example of the implications of this can be found in the evaluations recently done at Ohio State — evaluations which revealed that many students lack such basic knowledge as what constitutes a journal or an index. This means that without some instruction these students have little hope of utilizing library resources. In such instances, left to their own devices, students will borrow a book or two and write their papers with often outdated, inappropriate material, rather than use an effective search strategy approach to provide the most useful, relevant information for their needs. It also means that almost always a library instruction program must begin at the most rudimentary level.

The *B. I. Handbook* provides a needs assessment checklist (pp. 13-18); and three examples of needs assessment surveys are cited in Chapter Four of this handbook. Experts on surveys and needs assessment, who are often found in the sociology, psychology, and education departments, are also often available for consultation.

Goals and Objectives to Meet Needs

When needs have been identified, goals and objectives should be established to meet them. They must be clearly written and, very importantly, measurable. For example: library users need to learn how to use the computerized catalog at Ohio State University to locate books processed after Spring, 1982. An objective expressed as "students will learn to use the Library Control System (LCS) to find recently acquired books," is too vague because no specific skill or method is stated and it would be difficult to measure. A better way to state the objective would be: "students should be able to use LCS to access materials by author, title, and subject." This could then be broken down to such objectives as "students should be able to use the *Library of Congress Subject Headings (LCSH)* to identify and use the correct subject heading in doing an LCS subject search." The remainder of this chapter defines terms and explains characteristics of "good" goals and objectives; and provides many examples from experience in library instruction.

Goals

Goals are defined in the literature of education as either instrumental, (the means used to achieve terminal goals) or terminal (desired products or impacts). Evaluation thus can be undertaken on either the means of instruction or the product. In another sense, instrumental goals in higher education are desired inputs, while terminal "goals" are desired outputs of an institution. The *Dictionary of Education* defines goals as "a substance, object, or situation capable of satisfying a need and toward which motivated behavior is directed."(5) Goals are long-range and broad in scope and purpose; as contrasted with objectives, which are short-term, more specific, and "within reach." Goals provide the frame within which objectives are written. The *B. I. Handbook* states that a written statement of objectives should include immediate objectives and long-range goals, with timetables for implementation. One should remember to consult colleagues who are authorities in writing goals and objectives.

Robert Mager provides five steps in developing goals:

1. Write down the goal.

2. Write the performances that, if achieved, would achieve the goal.

3. Eliminate duplications and unwanted items.

4. Write a complete statement for each performance, including the nature, quality or amount acceptable.

5. Test the statements by determining that if the performances are achieved the goals will have been achieved.(6)

The LCS goal (stated previously), "Students should be able to use the *Library of Congress Subject Headings (LCSH)* volumes to identify the correct subject heading for doing an LCS subject search," would follow the five steps thus:

1. Students should be able to use *LCSH* to identify and use correct subject headings in doing an LCS subject search.

2. Students know how to use the *LCSH* to find the correct subject heading for their subject search. Students know how to do an LCS search by their subjects.

3. (Eliminate duplications or any unwanted words.)

4. Students identify the correct subject headings in *LCSH* for their assignments and write the subject headings on their papers. Students search LCS by their subjects and write down the first three titles listed under the subject.

5. Students write the correct subject headings on their papers thereby demonstrating their ability to choose the appropriate subject headings from the *LCSH*. Students write the first three titles listed under their subjects on LCS thereby completing a successful subject search of LCS using *LCSH*.

Fjallbrant and Stevenson point out that the goals and objectives of an instruction program must be in harmony with those of the larger institution, indeed with educational goals in general. They stress the importance of involving students and academic and library staff in the writing of goals and objectives, pointing out that each group will bring a different perspective to the task.(7)

Examples of goals statements in library instruction are: to provide a successful library experience to the user and to acquaint the beginning library user with the physical layout of the library. David King and John Ory have stated that the ultimate goals of library user education programs are to improve students' ability to use library resources and services effectively to meet their information needs and to instill in them realistic attitudes and expectations about the library and its accessibility.(8) Erland Nielson defines these goals as threefold:

1. that students recognize the need for library service;

2. that students develop systematic knowledge about their subject, its aids, and methodical literature searching; and

3. that students perceive the link between the library and their subject needs.(9)

Patricia Knapp urged that library instruction goals encompass "the whole range of knowledge and skills" that students need. She categorized them this way:

Students should

1. understand the nature and function of reference materials;

2. appreciate the value of the library as a source of information;

3. understand the nature and function of the bibliographical apparatus;

4. understand the function of literature-searching as a necessary step in problem-solving; and

5. be able to locate and select various kinds of library materials from the subject approach.(10)

The program written at the University of Texas at Austin places its goals in three categories: (1) user awareness; (2) orientation; and (3) bibliographic instruction. Goals are defined and objectives designed to meet the goals are enumerated; the examples of goals and objectives furnished in this document are very useful.(11) Another good example of established goals can be found in the goals statement written by the Penfield Library staff at SUNY Oswego. General goals of the library instruction program, in priority order, are:

1. that students learn to use basic library tools;

2. that students feel comfortable and competent in this library and thus will be more likely to use and support other libraries in the future;

3. that students use library services (reference help, interlibrary loan, computer data base searching, etc.) when appropriate for their disciplines;

4. that students learn how to use advanced library tools appropriate for their disciplines;

5. that there be improved relationships between librarians and students (i.e., contacts which are less anonymous); and

6. that faculty members improve their knowledge and use of library tools and services.

Objectives

The *Dictionary of Education* defines objective as an "aim, end in view, or purpose of a course of action or a belief" and behavioral objectives as "the aims or objectives of education stated as actual performance criteria or as observable descriptions of measurable behavior."(12) Robert Mager defines an objective as a "statement of intent that is specific enough to tell you "how to recognize one when you see one." It should clearly state "what the learner is expected to be able to do and how you will know when he is able to do it."(13) This is accomplished by defining expected performance; and Mager gives a good analysis of how this is done in his very readable book, *Measuring Instructional Intent.*

In his *Preparing Instructional Objectives,* Mager lists three characteristics of a useful objective:

1. performance (what the learner is able to do);

2. conditions (important conditions under which the performance is expected to occur); and

3. criterion (the quality or level of performance that will be considered acceptable).(14)

While these three criteria are useful, there are many specialists who do not believe that strict adherence to them is necessary. Their value is in reminding the evaluator that behavior, as well as content, should be measured. John Lubans identifies a complicating factor in establishing objectives for course-related library instruction. He points out that since course-related library instruction is not a discrete discipline, but integrated with instruction in an established discipline, its objectives must be clearly tied to course objectives.(15) Whereas the instructors make the final decisions on course goals and objectives, librarians need to insure that the instructors are familiar with the library program's goals and objectives.

Categories of Objectives

An understanding of the ways objectives may be categorized is useful. Vogel indicates the need to consider the two types of learning objectives — both the **cognitive** and the **affective**. Cognitive learning involves knowing, conceptualizing, and comprehending; affective learning involves attitudes and values. Emphasis in library instruction and education in general has been on cognitive learning evaluation. One interesting approach, the King and Ory study at the University of Illinois, concentrated on behavioral objectives — both cognitive and affective. The cognitive objectives included measuring the effect of instruction on student use of encyclopedias, bibliographies, etc. The affective (they called it "perceptual") evaluation measured the effects of instruction on "students' perceptions of the value of library instruction, their opinions about the library and confidence in their ability to use the libraries effectively."(16) They achieved this by measuring student responses to such statements as: everyone needs to know the library; using the library is a frustrating experience; I wish more information were available in how to do library research.(17)

Objectives, like goals, can be categorized as being either impact or process. Process objectives relate to the means used to achieve results, for example, teaching the use of the *Library of Congress Subject Headings (LSCH)* in a classroom presentation using transparencies and copies of pages from the volumes. Impact (or product) objectives relate to results; for example, a student is able to use *LCSH* to find the correct heading in the catalog. In brief, one knows that a process objective has been met when the lecture is finished, but one cannot determine if the impact objective has been achieved until it is ascertained whether the student actually can perform the function. The *B. I. Handbook* focuses primarily on impact objectives, as does this chapter.

In writing objectives one should consider the cognitive affective learning and the impact process principles. This will help to understand better what one wants to accomplish, to define it more clearly, and to be more comprehensive and thorough in one's planning. A very practical guide to writing goals and objectives is included in the *B. I. Handbook*. The handbook states that written objectives should:

> 1. include immediate and long-range goals with a timetable;
>
> 2. be directed to meet specific needs, and allow various methods of instruction for all in the academic community; and
>
> 3. include ways of measuring attainment of objectives, considering assessment of learning, attitude, and cost.(18)

The *B. I. Handbook* defines various types of objectives. The **general** objective is the overall goal of the instructional program; **terminal** objectives are specific and meaningful units which comprise the general objective; and **enabling** objectives define the specific knowledge or skills which are necessary to achieve the terminal objectives.(19) The handbook defines enabling objectives as behavioral in nature. Julie Vargas offers useful criteria for writing behavioral objectives:

> 1. be stated in terms of the student;
>
> 2. specify observable behavior;
>
> 3. indicate a level or criterion of acceptable performance; and
>
> 4. not contain any unnecessary words.(20)

General, Terminal, and Enabling Objectives

Some examples of general, terminal, and enabling objectives from the *B. I. Handbook* are useful for purposes of illustration. Note that the terminal objectives divide the general objectives into units and that the enabling objectives define how the terminal objectives can be achieved. (The complete list of objectives can be found on pp. 37-45 of the *B. I. Handbook*.)

General Objective: A student, by the time he or she completes a program of undergraduate studies should be able to make efficient and effective use of the available library resources and personnel in the identification and procurement of material to meet an information need.

Terminal: The student recognizes the library as a primary source of recorded information.

Enabling: When observed in real situations, students regularly turn to the library for needed information. These contacts include attempting to find information on their own using the appropriate library resources, and when that is not successful they contact a librarian.

Terminal: The student can make effective use of the library resources available to him or her.

a. She or he knows how to use institutional holdings records (such as the card catalogue and serials holdings list) to locate materials in the library system.

Enabling: Given a map of the library, the student can correctly identify the location of the library's catalogue (e.g., card catalogue, book catalogue, public shelf list) and other holdings lists in a specified period of time.

b. The student knows how to use reference tools basic to all subject areas.

Enabling: In a specified time period, the student can identify major reference tools (encyclopedia, dictionary, index) in a specified field using a guide to the literature such as *Sheehy's Guide to Reference Books.*

c. The student knows how information is organized in her or his own field of interest and how to use its basic reference tools.

Enabling: The student will identify the major channels of scholarly communication within her or his own field of interest and the formats in which this communication appears in the literature.

d. The student can plan and implement an efficient search strategy using library, campus, and other resources as appropriate.

Enabling: Given a complex topic in her or his own field of interest, in a specified time period, the student will indicate, orally or in writing: (1) the major subtopics involved; (2) whether the primary or secondary sources are required by each subtopic, and their general nature.

An example of the integration of terminal and enabling objectives into a program can be found at Brigham Young University. Five instructional programs were designed to meet the needs of all freshman and sophomore students. Terminal and enabling objectives were developed and test questions were created that would measure the objectives.(21) With a clear understanding of general, terminal, and enabling objectives, an examination of how objectives are classified becomes relevant.

Taxonomy of Educational Objectives

Because understanding both concept formation and creativity is so important in the setting of goals and objectives, a brief introduction to the content of Bloom's *Taxonomy of Educational Objectives* is useful. Bloom's work is helpful in formulating objectives by urging the writer to be more precise in using educational terms; he also provides examples of clarified objectives. He describes both cognitive and affective educational objectives and provides condensed versions of both the cognitive and affective taxonomies. Colleagues in education can be very helpful in applying Bloom's taxonomy to library instruction.

Since there has been much less evaluation done in the affective domain and cognitive learning is not only more easily measured but more applicable to library instruction, the focus here will be on the cognitive taxonomy. The six levels of the cognitive domain are; knowledge, comprehension, application, analysis, synthesis, evaluation. An example from the *B. I. Handbook* of the first level, **knowledge,** is:

> The student will be able to write these basic catalog filing rules:
>
> 1. the initial article is ignored in filing;
> 2. "Mc" is filed as if it were spelled "Mac;" and
> 3. numerals are filed as if spelled out.(22)

The second level is **comprehension,** which requires the student to restate or identify restatements of information in written or pictorial form. This includes paraphrasing, summarizing a statement, etc. An example would be: "The student will be able to summarize the filing rules in his own words."

The third level, **application,** requires that students be able to solve problems

different from those they have already seen. An example would be:
> The student will be able to find materials in the card catalog;
> 1. whose title begins with an article,
> 2. whose author's last name begins with "Mc" and "Mac," and
> 3. whose title begins with a numeral.

Analysis, the fourth level, requires of the student the ability to identify the component parts or structure of a whole. An example is: "the student will be able to identify the filing rules used in another index such as *Social Sciences Index, New York Times Index,* etc." (The student has applied filing rules as used in the card catalog; now he or she moves to the application of filing rules to all information seeking.)

The fifth level is **synthesis,** which is the ability to combine elements to make a unique product. An example from the handbook is "the student can plan and implement an efficient search strategy using library, campus, and other resources as appropriate."(23)

The sixth level, **evaluation,** is defined by Julie Vargas in *Writing Worthwhile Behavioral Objectives* as the "student tells whether or not a given product meets specified criteria or compares two products for some purpose and gives his reasoning."(24) An example from the *B. I. Handbook* is: "The student is able to evaluate materials and select those appropriate to his needs."(25)

Additional examples of the application to library instruction of Bloom's taxonomy and Vargas's criteria for writing behavioral objectives may help to clarify the various levels. Examples of **knowledge** objectives are:
> Students will be able to
> 1. write the major categories in the LC classification system;
> 2. describe the *LCSH* volumes and their usage; and
> 3. define the term "search strategy."

Examples of **comprehension** are: "Students will be able to describe search strategy in their own words, and describe a divided card catalog." **Application** examples are:
> Students will be able to
> 1. find the correct subject heading in *LCSH;*
> 2. use the card catalog to find material by author, title and subject; and
> 3. use the *Social Sciences Index* to find material by subject.

An example of **analysis** is: "The student will be able to outline a basic search strategy on a specific subject." An **evaluation** example is: "The student will be able to compile a bibliography, keeping a diary on how material is selected, eliminated, etc.''

Conclusion

Evaluating in terms of established goals and objectives helps to focus on what is needed, how that need can be met, and how successfully the need has been met. In preparing to evaluate library instruction in terms of established programmatic goals and objectives, one should begin by determining needs, and then set goals to meet those needs. General, terminal, and enabling objectives should be written — keeping objectives specific and meaningful. Finally, Bloom's taxonomy should be kept in mind to ensure that objectives are progressive in learning levels and comprehensive in their scope.

Suggested Reading

See Bibliography for full entry.

Bibliographic Instruction Handbook (1979)
Bloom (1956)
Fjallbrant (1978)
Mager (1972, 1973, 1975)
Vargas (1972)

Notes

1. *Bibliographic Instruction Handbook* (Chicago: American Library Association, 1979).

2. Michael Scriven in *Encyclopedia of Educational Evaluation: Concepts and Techniques for Evaluating Education and Training Programs* (San Francisco: Jossey Bass, 1975), p. 178.

3. J. Thomas Vogel, "A Critical Overview of the Evaluation of Library Instruction," *Drexel Library Quarterly,* No. 3 (1972), p. 315.

4. John Lubans, "Evaluating Library User Education Programs," in *Educating the Library User* (New York: Bowker, 1974), p. 234.

5. Carter V. Good, ed., *Dictionary of Education* (New York: McGraw, 1959), p. 262.

6. Robert Mager, *Goal Analysis* (Belmont, Calif.: Fearon Pitman, 1972), p. 72.

7. Nancy Fjallbrant and Malcolm Stevenson, *User Education in Libraries* (Hamden, Conn.: Linnet, 1978), pp. 19-20.

8. David King and John Ory, "Effects of Library Instruction on Student Research: A Case Study," *College and Research Libraries,* 40 (1981), 31.

9. Erland Kolding Nielson, "Aims and Objectives for User Education," NVBF Anglo-Scandinavian Seminar on Library Use, November 1976, p. 56.

10. Patricia Knapp, "A Suggested Program of College Instruction in the Use of the Library," *Library Quarterly,* 26 (1956), 226.

11. University of Texas at Austin, General Libraries, *A Comprehensive Program of User Education for the General Libraries, The University of Texas at Austin* (Austin, Texas: University of Texas, 1977).

12. Carter V. Good, pp. 392-393.

13. Robert Mager, *Measuring Instructional Intent* (Belmont, Calif.: Lear Siegler, 1973), p. 19.

14. Robert Mager, *Preparing Instructional Objectives* (Belmont, Calif.: Fearon, 1975).

15. John Lubans, "Objectives for Library User Instruction in Educational Media," in *Educating the Library User* (New York: Bowker, 1974), p. 212.

16. David King and John Ory, p. 34.

17. David King and John Ory, p. 38.

18. *Bibliographic Instruction Handbook,* p. 10.

19. *Bibliographic Instruction Handbook,* p. 44-45.

20. Julie S. Vargas, *Writing Worthwhile Behavioral Objectives* (New York: Harper and Row, 1972), p. 59.

21. Marvin E. Wiggins,"The Development of Library Use Instructional Programs," *College and Research Libraries,* 33 (1972), 473-479.

22. *Bibliographic Instruction Handbook,* p. 40.

23. *Bibliographic Instruction Handbook,* p. 43.

24. Julie Vargas, pp. 107-108.

25. *Bibliographic Instruction Handbook,* p. 43.

Bonnie G. Gratch was recently appointed as Coordinator of Bibliographic Instruction, Bowling Green State University Libraries. While a reference and instruction librarian at Drake Library, State University of New York, College at Brockport, she was involved in the development and evaluation of a two-semester, media-assisted basic library skills module in the General Education Program.

Chapter Three

Research Designs Appropriate for Evaluating Bibliographic Instruction

Bonnie G. Gratch

Introduction

This chapter will focus on research designs that involve particular kinds of planning efforts and methodologies for evaluating bibliographic instruction programs or components of programs. Since the subject of research design is a relatively complex issue in evaluation research, the information presented can be considered only as an introduction. However, numerous references are made to sources for more complete information, as well as the reminder to use local campus experts as resources.

Although there still continue to be differences of opinion among evaluation researchers about the benefits of experimental research designs, this chapter's primary focus is on some true experimental, quasi-experimental, and multiple-methods research designs. This focus is a deliberate one for three primary reasons:

1. Educational programs are quite different in their purpose and effects than social action or public policy programs; and therefore, research designs appropriate for evaluating educational programs should be distinguished from those used for evaluating social action programs. With that point in mind, many of the criticisms of experimental designs lose their force.

2. In order to adequately understand the issues and concepts of evaluation, a background in experimental research design is necessary as a springboard to understanding other possible designs.

3. Since one of the major reasons for conducting evaluations is to demonstrate causal relationships that lead to intelligent decisions, an understanding of the potential strengths and weaknesses of experimental designs is essential. In some cases an entire program has been eliminated as a result of negative findings based on invalid and unreliable data.(1)

To a lesser extent, this chapter also includes a section on survey research as a design alternative. A presentation of specific data collection methods are covered in the following chapter.

What is Research Design?

A research or evaluation design is a plan for how and when data will be collected for measurement purposes. It is important in order to improve the likelihood that causes of effects can be identified. As stated in the *Encyclopedia of Educational Evaluation:* "Evaluation...requires some kind of measurement or data collection. The conditions and scheduling under which the measures are taken or the data collected constitute the design of the evaluation study."(2) Often the concept of a research design is part of more formal, systematic evaluations of an entire instructional program or a component of an instructional program. However, research designs are also pertinent to studies comparing instructional methods or media.

Educational research and evaluation studies can be described by four broad types of research approaches:

1. descriptive studies often describing the status of a situation from information based on survey findings or direct observation;

2. causal-comparative method;

3. correlational method; and

4. the experimental method.

The following chart illustrates how the purpose of these approaches differ(3):

Research Approach	Purpose
Descriptive	To describe systematically the facts and characteristics of a given population or area of interest.
Causal-Comparative	To investigate cause-and-effect relationships by observing some existing consequence and searching back through the data for plausible causal factors.
Correlational	To investigate the extent to which variations in one factor correspond with variations in one or more other factors based on correlation coefficients (i.e., a statistical calculation).
True-experimental	To investigate possible cause-and-effect relationships by exposing one or more experimental groups to one or more treatment conditions and comparing the results to one or more control groups not receiving the treatment.
Quasi-experimental	To approximate the conditions of the true experiment in a setting which does not allow the control and/or manipulation of all variables.

Using a correlational approach, you might obtain two sets of scores: say, library assignment scores and scores based on an attitude survey that assessed how useful students believed the instruction session to be. These scores for the same group of students would then be used to compute a correlation coefficient; i.e., a descriptive statistic that indicates the magnitude of relationship between variables. Although the correlation coefficient would tell you the magnitude of the relationship, it cannot establish cause, although it may suggest causes in some cases. For examples of the correlational approach consult the Corlett study(4) and the Louttit study.(5)

In order to demonstrate causality between some kind of instructional activity and another condition or behavior, you would have to use an experimental method. This type of method involves manipulation of one variable and observation of its effect on another variable. For example, you could ask one group of teaching assistants to provide library instruction for one group of students and then compare the students' library assignment performance with a group that did not receive library instruction from their TA's. Assuming that other factors were controlled, a difference in performance between these two groups could be attributed to the library instruction.

Before examining more closely the characteristics of experimental designs, let's first focus on the importance of having a research design and the criteria for considering one or another design.

Why is a Research Design Important?

Every evaluator desires to increase confidence in his or her conclusions. A carefully conceived research design can directly contribute to an increase in confidence in your conclusions. The stronger the research design, the greater is your ability to assert cause and effect relationships. True experimental designs come the closest to allowing you to demonstrate a cause and effect relationship by permitting the acceptance or rejection of research hypotheses with little doubt that other variables might be responsible for the findings. And although opportunities for using true experimental research designs are somewhat limited in evaluating library instructional efforts, there are many solid designs which are superior to some currently being used and reported, and which, if used, would enhance your ability to demonstrate cause and effect relationships between library instruction and some post-instruction measure.

Assuming the importance of having a solid research design, the next questions are: how do you choose an appropriate design? and by what criteria do you assess one design over another?

Important Considerations in Choosing a Research Design
Purpose

The choice of a research design is directly dependent on the purpose of the evaluation. Here "purpose" has several meanings:

   1. Summative vs. formative evaluation: Naturally, if the purpose of the evaluation is to obtain feedback to be used to modify or improve an instructional activity, the choice of a design will be much different than if a summative evaluation is required which demands information about many impacts or that "proves" a program's effectiveness. In the former case, a simpler approach, perhaps utilizing

either a survey, true experimental, or quasi-experimental design would suffice. Whereas, in the latter case, a design encompassing a multiple methods approach known as "triangulation" (The word comes from navigation and surveying, and indicates that several different data sources are combined to zero in on the events being studied. It is used to overcome the biases and limitations of a single approach.(6)) might be more appropriate. Patricia Knapp and Nancy Fjallbrant are both two instruction librarians who have advocated evaluation studies with this type of multiple methods approach.(7, 8)

2. Program evaluation vs. evaluation of a program component, instructional mode, etc. Although the distinction here is similar to that in number one above, the main difference is one of magnitude and complexity. If two or more instructional modes are being evaluated in order to determine which is better meeting the instructional and affective objectives, a true or quasi-experimental design may be more appropriate than a survey design, but certainly a more sophisticated multiple methods approach is not required. However, to evaluate impacts of an entire instructional program, a multiple-methods approach is certainly called for.

3. Cognitive objectives and effects: The choice of a research design will definitely be influenced by the cognitive objectives. For example, an experimental design might be preferable to measure recall of content that is based on the cognitive objectives of the instruction program. On the other hand, a survey design would be more appropriate for measuring opinion, attitudes and perceptions that are based on the affective objectives of the program. And still some other research design or combination of methods might be warranted for measuring performance or process effects of the instruction.

Financial, Temporal, Political and Human Resources Considerations

The choice of a particular design is also dependent on the constraints of time, money, and human expertise. Probably the financial constraints are the most limiting, but academic librarians should never limit their horizons if in-house expertise is lacking. All campuses have faculty experts in educational and social science research who are usually willing to provide advice and technical assistance regarding choice of design, survey methodology or statistical analysis. It is particularly useful to tap these experts about statistical analysis options, because some of the weaker non-experimental designs can be strengthened to provide more reliable and valid data with the use of more sophisticated statistical analysis.

Nearly all evaluation studies take place under some sort of political or administrative "cloud." Being aware of the implications of this situation can have an effect on the choice of research design, its implementation, and the level of data analysis for an evaluation study. If quantitative "proof" is required by either the library or college administration, then a fairly strong experimental research design or a multiple methods approach is desirable.

And finally there is the advice of Suchman, a highly regarded writer and practitioner on this subject:

> There is no such thing as a single, "correct" design . . . Hypotheses can be studied by different methods using different designs.
>
> All research designs represent a compromise dictated by the many practical considerations that go into social research. None of us operate except on limited time, money and personnel. Further limitations concern the availability of data and the extent to which one can impose upon one's subjects. A research design must be practical.
>
> A research design is not a highly specific plan to be followed without deviation, but rather a series of guideposts to keep one headed in the right direction . . . Furthermore, any research design developed in the office will inevitably have to be changed in the face of field considerations.(9)

Beyond the considerations of purpose, financial, temporal, political and human resources, what must you keep in mind in order to intelligently choose one design over another? In other words, suppose the purpose of the evaluation suggests an experimental design, how will you select one experimental design over another? Or if you decide on a survey approach, what criteria need you be aware of in planning the survey?

Scientific Criteria of Relevance to Choice of Design

As much as possible, evaluation studies should seek to follow the scientific method of hypothesis testing used in other disciplines so that observation, description, and explanations of related events and cause and effect relationships will be based on empirical data of potential significance. Since the choice of a particular design will partially determine the quality of information obtained, it is important to realize that the information obtained from evaluation studies should meet as closely as possible the following scientific criteria:

> **Internal validity** — the information provided by the evaluation must display a reasonable correspondence to the phenomena which it purports to describe or interpret. An experimental design that used the scores of an achievement test to "prove" that students can successfully apply to a search strategy what they've learned in a lecture would most likely lack internal validity, since most achievement tests measure recall of discrete cognitive elements, rather than measure performance in using library resources.
>
> **External validity** — the information must be generalizable to similar situations beyond the one in which it was collected. That is, if five sections of 40 English 101 sections are evaluated on what they've learned in the freshman library skills program, the design used should allow you to generalize the findings to all 40 sections.
>
> **Reliability** — the information collected must be replicable. Repetition of the evaluation should produce essentially similar findings.
>
> **Objectivity** — the information collected must not be private in the sense that only particular persons would so interpret it.(10)

Experimental Research Designs

True experimental research is differentiated from other experimental methods by the concept of **control;** i.e., the evaluator specifies and controls the conditions that will occur in the evaluation, and the concept of **manipulating the treatment** (i.e., instruction) that is offered. But in order to fully understand experimental designs, certain concepts must be explained.

At least seven concepts are necessary: subjects, treatment, experimental group, control group, dependent variable, independent variables, control variables and intervening (sometimes called rival) variables. **Subjects** are the persons under study (although in other disciplines, non-human subjects, organizations or nation-states may be considered subjects). Subjects who will experience the proposed treatment or instruction are the **experimental group** and those subjects who will not experience the proposed treatment or instruction are the **control group.** A **treatment** is the condition that is applied to an experimental group, such as a library lecture, programmed instruction, etc. A **dependent variable** is the one you are interested in explaining; it is the measure of observable behavior of the subjects, such as attitude change, performance, use of a library, etc. An **independent variable** is the one used to explain one that is dependent and is frequently equated with the treatment. The independent variable is so-called because it is "independent" of the outcome itself. Instead, it is presumed to cause or effect the outcome. Also, the independent variable can be manipulated by the evaluator, such as offering bibliographic instruction to one group of subjects but not another group. **Control variables** are those that need to be controlled, held constant, or randomized so that their effects are neutralized, cancelled out, or equated for all conditions. Examples of control variables are age, sex, IQ, educational level, etc. When you are able to hold constant control variables, **control** is said to characterize the experimental situation. The concept of control is critical to experimental research and is the feature that distinguishes it from survey research.

One other component sometimes a part of experimental designs is the concept of **randomization.** Randomization ensures that two or more groups are as much alike as possible and that any difference is due to the independent variable and not to the differences among the subjects in the groups, such as sex, IQ, or motivational level. A distinction is often made between random **selection** and random **assignment.** Random selection means that each person in a defined population has an equal chance of being selected to take part in the study. Random assignment involves the random placement of subjects into an experimental or control group. Randomization is important to research design because using groups as similar as possible allows you to have more assurance that the instructional activity (the independent variable) is responsible for the difference(s) between groups as measured by the post-instruction measure (dependent variable).

Threats to Internal Validity

Additionally, you need to be aware of a number of threats or biases that affect the adequacy of a particular design. These threats or biases affect the validity of designs, thereby weakening the significance of the data obtained. Using an example, these threats to internal validity will be explained. Imagine an experimental situation in which you hypothesize that if social science graduate students receive instruction in how to use the *Social Science Citation Index (SSCI)* they will use it more often. You design an experiment for some social science graduate students in which one group receives an hour's training in the use of this index. The comparison group receives no training. The independent variable is characterized as training or no-training. Both groups of students are required to keep a record of how much time they spend using this index for two weeks after the training. These time records are the dependent variable.

In order to determine if use increased after training, you also asked students to keep time records two weeks prior to training. These pre-training records can be called a pretest.

You compute the statistics and find out that the results indicate a statistically significant increase in use by the experimental group, while the control group's use increased only a bit. The following are the threats to internal validity that weaken the validity of the conclusions:

1. Subjects — How do you know that the graduate students in the two groups weren't different in some important way before they received the training? This threat is related to **subjects** and can be corrected if the students are randomly assigned to the two groups, or some other measure applied to determine their equivalency.

2. History — How do you know that the students weren't influenced by other events occuring in their environment? For example, suppose some of the subjects in the experimental group had a library assignment in another course which required the use of the *SSCI*. This type of threat is referred to as **history.**

3. Maturation — Is there any psychological or biological change in the subjects which might provide an alternate reason for the experiment's results? Regarding the example, you could reason that graduate students must use the library a great deal and so would probably get to know about and use the *SSCI* anyway, regardless of training.

4. Mortality — Were subjects lost during the time of the experiment? For example, if three students dropped out of the experimental group, you could legitimately argue that these three may have been the ones not using the *SSCI*. If a specific type of subject drops out of the experiment, it could affect the results, and therefore be a threat to the validity of the findings.

5. Pretests — Does use of a pretest affect the dependent variable? For example, the time records the students kept before the training might have affected their behavior by focusing their attention on using the *SSCI*. Then, the **pretest,** rather than the independent variable might explain the experiment's results.

6. Measuring instruments — What if some of the students are just more conscientious about record keeping than others? Perhaps the use of time records is not a good measuring device. If the instruments used to measure the difference between experimental and control groups are inaccurate, the results could be explained by that factor, rather than by changes in the subjects.

7. **Extremes** — Selecting subjects on the basis of extremes can affect the results of a study. For example, if the subjects in the experimental group had all responded negatively on a library use questionnaire, they could be considered as reflecting an extreme. The study's findings would be subject to dispute because of a statistical effect called "regression." This effect results in the mean score always moving away from the extreme on a second test or second measure. This means that the use reported should increase anyway, regardless of the training.

8. **Interactions** — Are any of the above threats to internal validity interacting with another to produce an effect that might explain the study's results. For example, any of the **subjects** required to write research papers for other courses might interact with the **pretest** which focuses attention on the *SSCI*. This could result in increased use independent from the training.

Experimental research designs must be carefully planned so that as many as possible of these threats or possible explanations for supposed program effects can be controlled. The use of randomization and control groups, or more sophisticated kinds of statistical analyses, can control for many of these threats to internal validity. (Information for this section comes from Campbell and Stanley (11) and Cook and Greco.(12))

Threats to External Validity

Frequently we wish to generalize our findings to other groups or settings. Therefore, we must be concerned not only with threats to internal validity but also with threats to external validity. Now the issue becomes: Is there anything about the particular evaluation design that might make it inappropriate to assume that similar program effects would result in other situations? For example:

1. Has the setting for the evaluation study atypically affected the results? Is it artificial or atypical? This consideration becomes quite important, if you have created a laboratory-like environment for the experiment. Bibliographic instruction librarians usually don't have this problem, though, since most of our studies must take place in the "field," i.e., the library or classroom.

2. Are the subjects in the study similar in relevant characteristics to the population to which you wish to generalize? You probably should not be concerned with generalizing findings to any populations outside of your institution, but should be concerned that the subjects you use in a study do not differ on relevant characteristics from those to whom you wish to generalize. For example, you wouldn't want to use the results of a study using subjects enrolled in "honors" English sections to generalize to the freshman population.

As you can imagine, designs using a single group, such as the one-time case study or the one group pretest-post-test design are not recommended as appropriate models. The one time case study is characterized by an experimental treatment being administered to one group and then a post-test given to measure the effects of the treatment. The one group pretest-post-test design involves the administration of a pretest measuring the dependent variable, followed by the experimental treatment (i.e., the independent variable), and the final administration of a post-test measuring the dependent variable again. These are extremely weak "pseudo-experimental" designs because you will not be able to rule out most of the threats to internal or external validity.

Although libraries and classrooms are certainly not laboratories where conditions can be tightly controlled so that true experimental designs can always be used, this section will outline and illustrate three true experimental designs. The intent is to acquaint you with what is often regarded as the ideal in experimentation, and to point out the applications to evaluating bibliographic instruction, before introducing several quasi-experimental designs which may have wider applications to evaluating bibliographic instruction.

True Experimental Designs

Before describing specific designs, a brief explanation of commonly used symbols is necessary.

R denotes randomization; i.e., random assignment of subjects to groups. Also implied is that the subjects are randomly selected from the target population, although the classroom unit is frequently considered to be equivalent to the student population. There is some disagreement on this point, however. If you use the classroom unit as the sampling unit, then results can be generalized only to the classroom unit — e.g., freshmen English classes at Peoples College.

0 denotes the collection and measurement of data for the dependent variable from a group of subjects.

X (or Y or X_1, X_2) denotes the exposure of the group to the independent or treatment variable — the instruction.

The left to right dimension in a design diagram indicates the order in time of 0 and X. Also, different groups of subjects are distinguished by a different row of symbols for each group.

Design 1   Pretest-Post-test Control Group Design

| Experimental Group) | E: | R | 0_1 | X | 0_2 |
| (Control Group) | C: | R | 0_1 | | 0_2 |

Probably one of the most commonly used designs is the Pretest-Post-test Control Group Design. With this design there is one independent variable — the treatment — and one dependent variable. Subjects are assigned randomly to the control group and the experimental group. The dependent variable (called the pretest and designated by 0_1 in the diagram) is then measured for both groups. Then the treatment (the instruction which is designated by X) is given to the subjects in the experimental group only, after which the dependent variable is then measured again for both groups (the post-test which is designated by 0_2). The basic test of program effectiveness is indicated by the difference between 0_2 - 0_1 for each group.

If every effort is made to keep the E and C groups from having contact with each other, and if administration of the measures are as nearly comparable as possible for the two groups, this design rules out all of the threats to internal validity which were explained previously. However, this design does not always permit you to generalize the results to other students and settings. For example, it might be possible that the pretest sensitizes students in some unique way, so that evaluation results would not be replicated in a setting where no pretest is given. A couple of real studies reported in the library literature are used to illustrate this design. (All examples chosen for this chapter are for illustrative purposes only. The inclusion of a particular study should not be intepreted as a recommendation. For reviews and critiques of evaluation studies of bibliographic instruction, the reader is referred to the following articles listed in the ''Notes'' section at the end of this chapter: number 8 and numbers 13-17.)

Table 1 Pretest-Post-test Control Group Design

One large class, whose members were randomly assigned to E and C	E (24 Subjects)	R	O_1	X	O_2	
	C (26 subjects)	R	O_1		O_2	X

This study by Nagy and Thomas sought to evaluate the teaching effectiveness of two library instructional videotapes, a component of the instruction program.(18) The purpose was specifically to measure recall over a one-week time period of the content of two videotapes used to explain computer data base searching and research paper writing. Although the evaluation has several weaknesses, it does provide a good example of the pretest-post-test control group design and a way of surmounting the commonly made criticism about the improper use of denying treatment to a group for the sake of true experimental design. The design used follows the model except for the addition of the treatment (X) to the control group after the post-test and the experiment's completion. By allowing the control group to view the two videotapes after the completion of the experiment, no criticism can be levied regarding the issue of denying instruction for the sake of preserving the design's requirements.

Table 2 Variation on Pretest-Post-test Control Group Design

3 English Composition sections, students randomly assigned among the 3 groups	E1 (73 subjects)	R	O_1	X_1	O_2	O_2
	E2 (51 subjects)	R	O_1	X_2	O_2	O_3
	C (50 subjects)	R	O_1		O_2	O_3

The example represented in Table 2 represents a slight variation on this design as reported by Marvin E. Wiggins.(19) It illustrates how the design can be extended to cover more than one instructional aspect or mode, and in this case the use of two post-tests. The purpose of this summative evaluation was to prove that programmed instruction for teaching the use of the card catalog is more effective than a non-programmed alternative. The several objectives and hypotheses were carefully formulated, as was the development and refinement of the testing instrument. They effectively tapped local campus experts for guidance with sample sizes, randomization, test procedures and analysis of data.

E1 group received the programmed version (X_1), E2 the non-programmed (X_2), and C group received no instruction. Pretest and post-test (0_1 and 0_2) were similar examinations based upon the memorization of definitions and concepts. Post-test number 2 (0_3) required the subjects to make actual use of the card catalog.

Design 2   Pretest-Only Control Group Design

E: R X 0
C: R   0

This design is identical to the pretest-post-test control group design except that there is no pretest. According to the well-respected experimental researchers Campbell and Stanley, the use of a pretest is not actually essential to true experimental designs.(20) No pretest is used on the assumption that true random assignment of subjects to E and C groups ensures equivalence of the groups. In fact, the use of randomized assignment is a requirement for this design. This design is preferred if you are concerned about the possible effect of learning from the pretest. It is also much less time-consuming to administer and a less obtrusive method, since a measure is taken from both groups only once.

Table 3   Post-test-Only Control Group Design

200 science students	E1	R	X_1	0
randomly assigned	E2	R	X_2	0
	E3	R	X_3	0
	E4	R	X_4	0
	E5	R	X_5	0
	E6	R	X_6	0
	C	R		0

An example of this design using six experimental groups and one control group is illustrated in the excellent study by Kuo which investigated the relative effectiveness of different instructional modes as measured by a ninety-item objective test to assess recall of content.(21) The development and analysis of the testing instrument and the analysis of findings were carefully carried out. Because of the strength of the design and the rigorous procedures followed, the findings are valid and reliable.

Design 3   Solomon Four Group Design

E1	R	0_1	X	0_2
C1	R	0_1		0_2
E2	R		X	0
C2	R			0

The Solomon Four Group design, although the strongest of the true experimental designs, is much less frequently used because of its relative complexity and problems in administering. It utilizes two experimental and two control groups and is constructed in such a way that it has a number of checks that control for both random and systematic threats to internal and external validity. You would use this design if you really wanted to know if the pretest affects the post-test. By having the four groups you can compare the results for the two groups who experience both pretest and post-test to the two who only experience the post-test. A recently reported example of this design is the study carried out by Thomas Surprenant which compares programmed instruction to the lecture method.(22)

There are numerous variations or extensions of these design examples, usually involving the addition of one or more experimental and/or control groups. The reader is referred to the following sources in the "Notes" section: Huck(23), Stanley and Campbell(24), and Isaac and Michael(25). The common situation, however, makes it frequently impossible or infeasible to utilize true experimental designs, since bibliographic instruction librarians may lack control over when and/or which students are exposed to the treatment. Also, we often are limited to using intact classroom groups of students as subjects. In such situations the use of quasi-experimental designs are quite appropriate.

Quasi-Experimental Designs

Quasi-experimental designs are characterized by their attempts to approximate or simulate manipulation, providing certain controls and probing the data for causal dependencies. Although you do not have total control, you can control one or two of the following: when the observations are made, when the treatment or independent variable is applied, and which intact group receives the treatment. Only some examples will be presented here. You can obtain more examples by consulting the three references previously cited.(23-25)

Design 4   Non-Equivalent Control Group Design

$$E: \quad 0_1 \; X \; 0_2$$

$$C: \quad 0_1 \quad\;\; 0_2$$

(The dashes mean that the two groups are non-equivalent; i.e., they were not randomly selected and/or assigned.)

The Non-Equivalent Control Group design is a common one, since it is frequently utilized with intact groups, such as classes, because random assignment of subjects is not feasible. This design is similar to the Pretest-Post-test Control Group design (Design Number 1), except that subjects in the Non-Equivalent Control Group design are not assigned randomly from a common population to the two groups. This design is useful in confirming or ruling out some plausible intervening and control variables when use of a true experimental design is not possible. The more similar the E and C groups are in their recruitment, and the more this similarity is verified by pretest scores, the more effective this control becomes. This design can also be used when two treatments are used and with more than two groups. However, since students are not assigned randomly, there are more threats to the internal validity of the conclusions. Since the groups are non-equivalent on an unknown number of variables, it is possible (though not always plausible) that there is some interaction between X and variables specific to the experimental group. The equivalence of the groups cannot be assured by matching, and statistical procedures such as analysis of covariance and regression do not necessarily provide the proper adjustment for those variables on which the experimetal and control groups differ, but many evaluation experts still advocate its utility. In fact, this design may have an advantage over the true experimental designs because it can control for subject reactivity; that is, subjects are much less likely to be aware of participating in an experiment when they are not manipulated by their assignment into E and C groups. For an example of an improved version of this design, see Eash.(26)

Examples of this design in the library literature are relatively common; see for example, Hardesty(27), Phipps(28), Eyman(29), and Stewart(30). The Hardesty, Lovrich and Mannon study is used here chiefly because it also illustrates careful test development.

Table 5 Non-Equivalent Control Group Design				
262 Freshman students enrolled in several English composition courses	E (133 subjects)	0_1	X	0_2
	C (129 subjects)	0_1		0_2

All 262 freshmen were given the evaluation instrument as a pretest. This instrument was carefully developed to meet the criteria of validity and reliability. During the course of the semester, 133 subjects received the instruction from reference librarians. Two separate classes (129 subjects) served as the control group and received no library instruction of which the evaluators were aware. Then, eight weeks later, all 262 subjects were given the original test. In addition to the way the limitations inherent in this design affect the validity of the findings, you must also be concerned with the appropriateness of using this design as the basis for a summative evaluation. Unless used in combination with other techniques, causality may be difficult to ascertain.

A variation on this design, called by Campbell and Stanley "patched-up," assumes that there are two student groups judged to be roughly comparable, and that one of these groups has just received the instructional activity and the other is about to be exposed to it.(31) For example:

E_1 X 0_1
E_2 0_1 X 0_2

If the instructional activity has had an effect, it will be confirmed by the following positive differences: 0_1 for the first group will be greater than 0_1 for the second group, and 0_2 will be greater than 0_1 for the second group. Also, the difference between 0_2 for the second group and 0_1 for the first group provides information about the effects of the pretest on the post-test.

Time-Series Designs

Time-series designs, types of quasi-experimental designs, involve repeated observations or measurements on some group or individual before and after treatment. There are single-group time-series designs and multiple-group ones. A longitudinal study is a type of time-series design which involves repeated measure of the same subjects. For example:

Design 5   Longitudinal Study

0_1 X 0_2 X 0_3 0_4

The above represents the simplest form of this design. It is appropriate when there is concern for continuous monitoring of an ongoing program or with long-term program effects. There is no set number of required observations (0's) or treatments (X's). There are some threats to internal and external validity with the simple form of this design; however, an improvement is obtained by adding a control group or groups. For example:

E: 0_1 X 0_2 X 0_3 X 0_4
C: 0_1 0_2 0_3 0_4

By adding a control group, the threat of history is controlled, as well as other threats to external validity.

An alternative strategy which controls for the same threats to validity, as well as offering other advantages is the following:

E1: 0_1 X 0_2
E2: 0_1 X 0_2
E3: 0_1 X 0_2
E4: 0_1 X 0_2

These groups are all pretested at the same time, but are post-tested at different intervals of time. This strategy is particularly useful where maturational factors are involved and where the effects of serial testing within groups should be minimized.

There are certainly many other research designs that could be considered, but what must be emphasized is that there is never a perfect design, nor can all of our evaluation needs in bibliographic instruction meet the requirements of true experimental designs. Therefore, when an experimental approach seems appropriate and a true experimental design is impossible, an attempt to use the best possible quasi-experimental design should be made. But, if you are faced with using a fairly weak quasi-experimental design of which the findings are subject to a variety of interpretations, then you should carefully consider the use of a multiple-methods approach which will provide a broad range of data from multiple sources. Certainly when a major, summative evaluation of an entire program is required, a multiple-methods approach is desirable. The following examples serve to illustrate this approach.

Multiple Methods Approach

An excellent example of this approach for a summative evaluation is the Kirk study whose purpose was to compare the lecture-demonstration method to the guided exercise method of instructing students in an introductory biology class.(32) The purpose of the study was to measure the effectiveness of a library instruction technique designed to teach students a process and to influence their library use behavior. The multiple-methods research approach combined the post-instruction data-gathering techniques of testing, attitude assessment via a questionnaire, and the unobtrusive method of analysis of bibliographies. It can be represented as:

190 students in a	E1:	X	0_1	0_2	0_3	0_4
general biology class	E2:	Y	0_1	0_2	0_3	0_4

The two groups were formed on the basis of enrollment in separate laboratory sections. A pretest on general library skills learned in high school was administered to determine if the two groups were essentially similar. Both groups were then given library instruction during the first week of classes, which was either a two-hour lecture/demonstration (X), or a guided exercise done by the students individually at their own speed (Y). Identical information was presented in both forms of instruction. The post-instruction measures for the dependent variable included: an essay question that required library research and resulted in the writing of papers with bibliographies; librarian evaluation of a randomly selected sample of bibliographies (0_1); two library tests (0_2); a student attitude assessment instrument (0_3); and finally the biology faculty-developed student attitude assessment instrument (0_4).

A final example of the multiple-methods approach is the evaluation studies of a user education program carried out by Nancy Fjallbrant at Chalmers University of Technology Library, Sweden. Her overall design was a series of evaluations of all the components of the user education program "in order to produce a triangulation effect and thereby obtain as full a picture as possible."(33) She combined experimental design methods with survey and unobtrusive methods for the purposes of evaluating content learning, student and faculty attitudes about specific instructional activities, and students' application of content and their performance in using the library. She also combined one-time designs with longitudinal designs.

The following brief section devoted to survey research is provided to draw attention to this method as a design alternative. More information about survey research can be found in the next chapter.

Survey Research

Survey research is characterized by:

> 1. the selection of representative, random samples of persons, objects, etc. from pertinent populations;

> 2. questioning and examining these samples through interviews, questionnaires, attitude tests or observation in order to obtain information about a research problem or to test hypotheses;

> 3. analysis of data to explain behavior or events, or how certain variables are related.(34)

Survey research, by itself, is usually not appropriate for demonstrating causal relationships; instead, it is more effectively used for obtaining descriptive and attitudinal information about existing library practices, activities, services, etc., as well as establishing correlational relationships between variables.

Some examples of research questions that could be addressed by using survey research methods are:

> 1. determining whether recipients of instruction are pleased with the instruction;

> 2. assessing the general awareness of and the degree to which an instruction program and its components are used;

> 3. determining the information-gathering behavior of library users;

> 4. finding out about the kinds of information needed by library users and non-users, as well as the types of sources used;

> 5. determining the perceptions of recipients of instruction about what they've learned and how it has affected them.

Summary

This chapter has primarily focused on experimental research designs because of their ability to demonstrate causal relationships. However, other approaches, which are sometimes combined when evaluating components of an entire instruction program, are extremely useful. These approaches include survey research, correlational methods, causal-comparative methods, and others not treated in this chapter. When used together for the purpose of evaluating an entire instructional program a multiple methods approach results. This kind of approach can be extremely effective in providing valid and reliable information about your bibliographic instruction activities.

But, what are the important questions you need to consider when choosing one approach over another, or one experimental design over another?

1. What is the purpose behind your evaluation?

2. Do you only want to describe your first year's activities with some feedback from program participants?

3. Or do you want to assert that program participants actually learned X or can now perform Y as a result of library instruction?

4. Or do you want to demonstrate that the revised version of your workbook or the use of audio/visual aids has positively affected the students' ability to do X or Y?

Remember, if you are interested in describing activities or attitudes, consider a survey approach or information based on your observations and/or program participants' observations. If you want to demonstrate that certain relationships exist, consider a correlational or a causal-comparative approach. If, however, you want to assert that a particular instructional activity or medium caused a certain behavior or change in program participants, then an experimental design is recommended.

Your next question might be: "How do I choose one experimental design over another?" Naturally, there are important practical considerations such as available financial and human resources. Some of the experimental designs highlighted in this chapter require more time and expertise to plan, administer and analyze the resulting data than other designs. Also, you must consider the limitations at your institution that affect your ability to carry out true experimental designs. For example, you may not be able to control which students are used in the study. If that is the case, you cannot randomly assign subjects to groups. Therefore, you will have to use a suitable quasi-experimental design.

Since there are so many considerations to a choice of an overall approach or a choice of one experimental design versus another, the information provided in this chapter can only be considered as a beginning resource. Naturally, you will want to consult some of the cited references for further information. We also strongly recommend your seeking assistance from campus experts in departments of sociology, educational research, or psychology.

While this chapter has examined a variety of plans or designs for how and when data are collected, it has not discussed data gathering instruments. The next chapter will discuss several instruments, focusing particularily on tests and questionnaires.

Research Designs 59

Notes

1. David H. Eyman and Alvin C. Nunley, *The Effectiveness of Library Science 1011 in Teaching Bibliographical Skill* (Talequah, Okla.: Northeastern Oklahoma State University, 1977), (ERIC ED 150 962).

2. S. B. Murphy, et. al, *Encyclopedia of Educational Evaluation* (San Francisco, Calif.: Jossey Bass, 1975), p. 122.

3. Stephen Isaac and William B. Michael, *Handbook in Research and Evaluation*, 2d ed. (San Diego, Calif.: Edits Pub., 1981), p. 42.

4. Donna J. Corlett, "Library Skills, Study Habits, Attitudes, and Sex as Related to Academic Achievement," *Educational and Psychological Measurement*, 34 (1974), 967-969.

5. C. M. Louttitt and James R. Patrick, "A Study of Students' Knowledge in the Use of the Library," *Journal of Applied Psychology*, 16 (1932), 475-484.

6. Miriam Lewin, *Understanding Psychological Research* (New York: John Wiley and Sons, 1979), p. 9.

7. T. D. Cook and D. T. Campbell, "The Design and Conduct of Quasi-Experiments and True Experiments in Field Settings," in *Handbook of Industrial and Organizational Psychology*, ed. R. Dunnette (Chicago, Illinois: Rand McNally, 1976), pp. 223-326.

8. Nancy Fjallbrant, "Evaluation in a User Education Programme," *Journal of Librarianship*, 9 (April 1977), 83-95.

9. Edward A. Suchman, "General Considerations of Research Design," as stated in *Handbook of Research Design and Social Measurement*, ed. D. Miller (New York: David McKay, 1970), p. 40-41.

10. Egon G. Guba and D. L. Stufflebeam, *Evaluation: The Process of Stimulating, Aiding, and Abetting Insightful Action* (Bloomington, Indiana: Indiana University, 1970), p. 33-34, (ERIC ED 055 733).

11. Donald T. Campbell and Julian C. Stanley, "Experimental and Quasi-Experimental Designs for Research on Teaching," in *Handbook of Research on Teaching*, ed. N. L. Gage (Chicago: Rand McNally, 1963), p. 171-246.

12. Kenneth Cook and C. M. Greco, "The Ugly Duckling Acknowledged: Experimental Designs for Decision-Making - Part I," *Journal of Academic Librarianship*, 3 (March 1977), 23-28; and "Part II," 3 (May 1977), 85-89.

13. James G. Brewer and P. J. Hills, "Evaluation of Reader Instruction," *Libri*, 26 (March 1976), 56-64.

14. Thomas G. Kirk, "Bibliographic Instruction: A Review of the Research," in *Evaluating Library Use Instruction*, ed. Richard J. Beeler (Ann Arbor, Michigan: Pierian Press, 1975), pp. 1-30.

15. Richard H. Werking, "Evaluating Bibliographic Instruction: A Review and Critique," *Library Trends*, 29 (Summer 1980), 153-172.

16. Arthur P. Young and E. B. Brennan, "Bibliographic Instruction: A Review of Research and Applications," in *Progress in Educating the Library User*, ed. John Lubans, Jr. (New York: Bowker, 1978), pp. 13-28.

17. Arthur P. Young, "Research on Library User Education: A Review Essay," in *Educating the Library User,* ed. John Lubans, Jr. (New York: Bowker, 1974), p. 242-246.

18. Laslo A. Nagy and Martha L. Thomas, "An Evaluation of the Teaching Effectiveness of Two Library Instructional Videotapes," *College and Research Libraries,* 42 (1981), 26-30.

19. Marvin E. Wiggins, "Evaluation in the Instructional Psychology Model," in *Evaluating Library Use Instruction,* ed. Richard Beeler (Ann Arbor, Michigan: Pierian Press, 1975), pp. 89-96.

20. Donald T. Campbell and Julian C. Stanley, p. 195.

21. Frank K. Kuo, "A Comparison of Six Versions of Science Library Instruction," *College and Research Libraries,* 34 (1973), 287-290.

22. Thomas T. Surprenant, "Learning Theory, Lecture, and Programmed Instruction Text: An Experiment in Bibliographic Instruction," *College and Research Libraries,* 43 (1982), 31-37.

23. Schuyler Huck, W. H. Cormier, and W. G. Bounds, Jr., *Reading Statistics and Research* (New York: Harper & Row, 1974), Chapter 13.

24. Donald T. Campbell and Julian C. Stanley.

25. Stephen Isaac and William B. Michael, Chapter 3.

26. Maurice J. Eash, et. al, *Evaluation Designs for Practitioners — TM Report No. 35* (Princeton, New Jersey: ERIC Clearinghouse on Tests, Measurements and Evaluation, 1974), p. 3 (ERIC ED 150 962).

27. Larry Hardesty, Nicholas P. Lovrich, Jr., and Jame Mannon, "Evaluating Library Use Instruction," *College and Research Libraries,* 40 (1979), 309-317.

28. Shelly Phipps and Ruth Dickstein, "The Library Skills Program at the University of Arizona: Testing, Evaluation, and Critique," *Journal of Academic Librarianship,* 5 (September 1979), 205-214.

29. David H. Eyman and Alvin K. Nunley.

30. Barbara C. Stewart, *An Evaluation of a Course in Library Instruction at Ball State University* (ERIC ED 138 246).

31. Donald T. Campbell and Julian C. Stanley, pp. 227-229.

32. Thomas Kirk, "A Comparison of Two Methods of Library Instruction for Students in Introductory Biology," *College and Research Libraries,* 32 (1971), 465-474.

33. Nancy Fjallbrant, p. 90.

34. Charles Busha and Stephen P. Harter, *Research Methods in Librarianship* (New York: Academic Press, 1980), p. 88.

Mignon S. Adams is Coordinator of Information Services at Penfield Library, State University of New York at Oswego. She has been involved in the development of an instructional program for the past ten years and has given a number of presentations on evaluating bibliographic instruction.

Chapter Four

Data Gathering Instruments

Mignon S. Adams

A key part of the evaluation process is gathering the data which will be analyzed. This chapter is concerned with the variety of instruments (tests, assignments, questionnaires, interviews, scales, etc.) which may be used to collect information.

Choosing an Instrument

Purpose.

The first step in choosing an instrument to gather data is to decide upon the purpose for the instrument. You may want to determine what students presently know; in which case, a "pretest" may be called for. A pretest may be used to identify those students who do not have necessary background knowledge. For example, the student who doesn't know where the call number is located on a catalog card will need more instruction than those who do know. A pretest can also measure the content you intend to teach; if most of the students can already meet your objectives you will want to change the content of your instruction.

After instruction, you will want to know whether students have mastered the content of the instruction. If you are teaching a credit course, you must also have a basis for assigning grades. "Post-tests," based upon the objectives of the instruction, are the most commonly used. If the same instrument is used for both a pretest and a post-test, the difference in scores can be examined to see what students learned. This procedure is often used in research designs.

Besides asking if students have met objectives, you may have other questions to be answered. For example, did student behavior change (for example, do they now use more efficient techniques for library research)? In that case, "performance measures" (which could be either pre- or post-test measures) would be the appropriate tools. What do students feel or think about the instruction or the program? You can ask them, either through a questionnaire or an interview. What are student attitudes towards the library? Asking students to respond to an "attitude scale" can answer this question.

Available resources.

After deciding what you want your instrument to measure, you will need to examine available resources. Your time is important. Many measures, such as essay tests or interviews, can be very time-consuming. Constructing any good instrument takes a great deal of time. Clerical support is also important, since tests and questionnaires must be typed, reproduced, and scored.

If you are testing large numbers of students, you should certainly consider computer scoring, which will affect the types of questions you ask. Most academic computer centers have standard programs for scoring tests and scales. Check with your local center for format requirements, available statistical packages, and turn-around time. If you do not use computer scoring, pay careful attention to the layout of your instrument. For example, placing blanks for answers down the left-hand side of the page rather than having students circle answers in the middle of the page can save hours of scoring time.

You must also determine if you may be permitted access to students. In course-related instruction, the time you have available for testing is dependent upon the willingness of the course instructor. Therefore, you may need to use instruments which do not take a considerable amount of class time.

A final resource is the availablility of consultant help on your campus. Some institutions have professional development centers, part of whose task is to help faculty develop evaluation tools. However, any campus with education, psychology, or sociology departments has people whose area of expertise is in testing and evaluation. An hour spent reviewing your instrument with one of these people can save you from embarrassing mistakes. To locate help, look to see who teaches such courses as "Tests and Measurements," "Evaluation Techniques," or "Research Methods."

Library Skills Tests (Paper and Pencil)

The term "paper-and-pencil-test" refers to tests which are taken sitting down, responding silently to written questions. They are the most commonly-used measuring instruments in education, so it's not surprising that they are often used to measure library skills. These tests are usually easy to administer, large numbers of students can take them, and they can be easily scored.

Standardized tests are often used in education for diagnostic purposes (e.g., reading readiness), measuring achievement (the *Iowa Basic Skills Tests*) or judging aptitude (the SAT or GRE). "Standardized" usually means that a test has been carefully constructed by experts, has directions for administering the test in a standard manner, and has tables of norms.(1) A table of norms is prepared by administering a test to a large number of representative students, so that you can compare the scores your students achieve with the scores obtained by students of the same grade level.

In addition, a good standardized test (as with any good test) has demonstrably high validity and reliability. "Validity" refers to whether or not the test results measure what they were intended to measure. If a library test purports to measure the ability to use a library effectively, then an effective library user should score high on it. "Reliability" refers to whether or not the test is consistent over a period of time. The witness in a courtroom who consistently tells the same story is reliable—but he or she may not be telling the truth and thus the evidence given may not be valid.(2) Validity and reliability may both be tested statistically (see any basic statistics text), and results of these tests should be contained in the manual of a standardized test.

There are not many standardized library tests. The publishers of all eleven listed in the latest *Mental Measurements* and *Tests in Print* were contacted in 1982. Only one publisher still had a test in print. The only widely-used tests for college students, the *Peabody Library Information Test* and *A Library Orientation Test for College Freshmen* (often referred to as the Feagley test), have been out-of-print for some time. Masse Bloomfield has discussed the Feagley test, and it has been reprinted.(3)

Five tests were located which were available in 1982:

Bennett, Alma and H.E. Schrammel. *Bennett Use of Library Test.* High
school and college. Bureau of Educational Measurements, Kansas State
Teachers College, Emporia, KS 66801, 1947.

Somewhat standardized directions; normed on "students in classes studying Library Science"; manual gives information on internal reliability; two
different forms available. Consists of 130 questions concerning parts of books,
use of card catalog, Dewey Decimal system, terms, choice of reference books,
and periodical entries. The test has evidently not been updated since 1947.
Some answers are no longer correct, and typographical errors make others
incorrect. Many of the items are ambiguous or poorly-worded.

Nationwide Library Skills Examination. Gr. 4-12. Educational Stimuli,
Telegram Building, Superior, WI 54880, 1963.

Somewhat standardized directions; normed on 8500 students, grades 4-12,
from across the country; no information given on validity or reliability. Consists of 100 questions. Thirty of these are on parts of a book or abbreviations
found in books; twenty more are on alphabetization; ten questions each are
devoted to selecting the right reference book for certain information and for
the Dewey major classifications; five questions each on identifying parts of
a catalog card and interpreting periodical entries. Many of the items are obscure;
librarians either couldn't answer them or couldn't agree on the right answer.

Hyland, Anne M. *The Ohio School Library/Media Test. Gr. 4-12.* The
Author, 236 E. Clearview, Worthington, OH 43085, 1978.

Standardized directions; normed on 2670 Ohio students, grades 4-12; manual
gives information on content and construct validity. Consists of 53 questions,
based on objectives in curriculum guides, and professional judgements.
However, since one-fourth of the questions deal with how to use media,and
another small group with reading and picture comprehension, the test is probably of limited use to academic librarians. Questions are generally well-written
(there was only one the sample of librarians couldn't answer), and there are
a number of questions which test for more than simple recall.

*Iowa Tests of Educational Development: Test SI, Use of Sources of In-
formation. Gr. 9-12.* 7th ed. Science Research Associates, 155 North
Wacker Drive, Chicago, IL 60606, 1979.

Standardized directions; normed on high school students around country;
validity and reliability information available; two different forms. Consists

of 69 questions, 47 on the "mechanics of use," including books, card catalog, periodicals and indexes, and reference works; and 22 questions on "evaluation of sources," which ask students to select the best or more likely source of information on a given problem. (Many of these are not library sources.) Questions are clearly written, and concentrate on solving information problems rather than on terms or identifying parts of a catalog card or entries.

Illinois Association of College and Research Libraries. Library Skills Test. Gr. 7-12, plus 13. Scholastic Testing Service, Bensenville, IL 60106, 1980.

Standardized directions; normed on 3,000 high school students from seven states, and 1,200 Illinois college freshmen; reliability information in manual. Consists of 45 questions developed by six academic librarians. 21 questions ask for definitions; 17 are on interpreting a catalog card or an index entry; four on call number arrangement; and two on distinguishing bibliographic forms. Questions are generally clear, but all but three test only simple recall. Academic librarians could use this as a pre-test to ascertain that students know terminology and how to interpret entries, but the items are too easy to be able to discriminate much among college freshmen—and, in fact, when the testing was done on college freshmen, almost half the questions were answered correctly by 85% or more of the students.

Locally-produced tests would still be necessary even if there were many standardized library tests available. Tests that you design yourself measure your objectives, and your emphases. However, writers on test construction are in agreement that teacher-made tests are of generally low quality. Librarian-made tests often exhibit the same faults test experts assign to teacher-made tests. The tests tend to be poorly-written (ambiguous, items given not clearly right or wrong), and hastily prepared; they tend to test for low-level objectives only (simple recall of fact) and dwell on trivia (for example, concentrating on dates and definitions).

Steps in test construction.

In general, the steps in test construction recommended by commonly-used test textbooks (4) are these:

l. Decide upon the purpose.

You may want to identify those students who need remedial help, find out if students have mastered objectives, or be able to rank students (for example, in order to assign grades).

2. Determine the skills or knowledge you want to measure.

If you do not know what you want to measure, you may well wind up measuring nothing at all.

3. State these skills or knowledge specifically enough to be able to write test items.

This step does not mean that writing behavioral objectives is essential. However, writing down what the student is expected to know or do helps you concentrate on what is important and testable. For example, a common library test question is:

The card catalog is:
A. Not divided. B. Divided into 2 parts. C. Divided in 3 parts.

The implied objective for this question is: Students will be able to state how many parts the card catalog is divided into. A more important objective might be: Students will look in one place for subjects, another for titles. This objective indicates a different test item. Writing specific objectives or skills will help you avoid unimportant test items.

4. Prepare a table of specifications.

A table of specifications is like a blueprint or outline of a test. For each objective to be covered, you should decide how many test items are to be written. This ensures that all content areas are covered appropriately, since you probably don't want 20 questions on alphabetization and only five on periodical indexes.

Also important is that your plan calls for testing several levels of objectives. While librarians often state that an instructional objective is to teach students how to develop efficient search strategies, their tests tend to test students only on whether or not they can identify parts of a catalog card or interpret an index entry.

Writers on test construction stress using some form of Bloom's taxonomy of objectives (discussed in Chapter 3) to help in writing questions which test for higher-level objectives. Here are some examples of objectives based on Bloom's hierarchy with examples of test items:

Knows general terms:

Objective: Student will know that periodical is another name for a magazine or journal.
Test item: Another name for a magazine or journal is:
A. A digest. B. A periodical. C. An abstract. D. An index.

Understands principles and generalizations.

Objective: Student will understand the reasons for using a specialized index.

Test Item: You would use a special index such as the *Social Sciences Index* when you want to:

    A. Locate information quickly on a topic you don't know anything about.
    B. Find scholarly information on a topic.
    C. Find a general magazine article on a topic.
    D. Locate addresses of social scientists.

Applies principles and generalizations.

Objective: Student can select an appropriate index to locate information in scholarly journals.

Test item: You have found an article suitable for your topic in the *Journal of Studies on Alcohol.* You will be most likely to find a similar article by looking in:

    A. The card catalog
    B. *Readers' Guide*
    C. *Social Sciences Index*
    D. *Humanities Index*

(**Note:** If during your class, you taught that students should look in the *Social Sciences Index* to find articles similar to the ones in the *Journal of Studies on Alcohol,* then of course the above question deals only with recall. If the student has to conclude that this journal is a scholarly one, and deals with the social sciences, then the question tests for application of principles.)

5. Decide upon a format for the test questions.

If you are dealing with a large number of students, you will probably choose an objective form which can be machine-scored. While only essay tests measure the abilities to write and to organize ideas, carefully-written multiple-choice items can measure high-level objectives.

6. Write test items.

It is difficult to write good test items, and even more difficult to write good test items which test for more than recall of knowledge. Any of the standard test textbooks listed in the bibliography give instruction and examples of constructing test items, ranging from short-answer through multiple-choice to essay questions.

7. Have a colleague react to test items.

Once test items are written, never fail to have someone else react to them. Questions which seem perfectly obvious to you may turn out to have several different correct answers. Here are some examples:

Poor:

    You can find periodical articles by looking in:

      ("The library" is a correct answer, among many others.)

A little better, but not much:

> You can find periodical articles by using:
>
> (Periodicals?)

Improved:

> The most-often used index for finding general periodical articles is called:
>
> (*Readers' Guide* is the only correct answer.)

Use your computer center to perform standard statistical measures. Your computer center is more than likely to be able to quickly score your tests for you, as well as give you statistics and perform an item analysis so that you know if there are questions which should be discarded.

Performance Measures

> *Paper and pencil tests measure whether the pupil knows or understands what to do when confronted with a problem situation but cannot determine what the pupil will do. (5)*

If you want to know if you have actually changed student behavior, you will have to develop other measures than a paper and pencil test. A number of performance measures have been used in bibliographic instruction.

Simulated experiences.

If you can set up a problem which closely approximates a real situation, you have a better idea of what students will do.

Worksheets are often used in credit courses and course-related instruction to simulate actual library experience. The workbook developed by Miriam Dudley (6) at UCLA, for example, was designed to be used by large numbers of students and is easily scored. The workbook consists of some 20 worksheets which ask students to perform such skills as locating subjects in the card catalog and locating answers to questions in appropriate reference books.

Worksheets can also be developed which use student choice of topic. For example, using their own topics, students can be asked to select an appropriate periodical index, find a suitable article, and determine whether or not the library owns the periodical in which the article appears. Such worksheets have the advantage of being more pertinent to the student and can be only slightly more time-consuming to check. Instruction programs have used such worksheets with as many as 500 students a semester.

Again, worksheets will not tell you what students will do in a completely unstructured situation. But because students can be asked to perform in a way which approximates unstructured situations, you may have a clearer idea of what they will do in real life than from a sit-down test. Like a test, worksheets may ask only for low-level objectives to be met ("write down the call number," "find this subject heading") or also for higher-level ones ("choose an appropriate index," "write down all the places in the library you could find information on this topic"). And, like test items, worksheets must be carefully constructed to avoid ambiguous wording and confusing directions.

A complex performance test was devised by Patricia Knapp and her staff at Monteith College.(7) The test asked students to find entries in the card catalog and a periodical index; select the most useful books from among many listed under a heading in the card catalog; use surface clues to evaluate books; use an annotated bibliography; and develop a search strategy. While the test, administered over a two-day period, is too time-consuming for most librarians to use with more than a few students, the description of the test and its development of objectives could be helpful for anyone designing performance tests.

Finally, class assignments are often given as simulated experiences. Case studies, problems, projects, are all ways in which students can be asked to respond as they would in a real situation.

Reports by students.

Another way to determine what students will do is to ask them what they have done in a real situation. For example, librarians at the University of Illinois asked both control and experimental groups of freshmen what sources and library services they used to write their research papers.(8) Students may also be asked to keep a diary or journal of their research. A composition teacher at SUNY/Oswego assigns his students a short paper which describes their reaction to writing the research paper (after finishing it) and using the library. Students may also be interviewed; but because interviewing is a time-consuming process, it will probably be possible to interview only a small number.

Remember that if students are to respond truthfully, it is imperative that they know their responses will in no way affect their grades and that their answers will be kept anonymous or at least confidential.

Analysis of products.

You can also determine what students have done by examining what they have produced. One procedure is to look at the bibliographies of their research papers. You may want to look for varieties of materials used (books, periodicals, government documents, etc.) and at levels (popular sources versus scholarly ones). Interviews with instructors on their perceptions of the quality of the papers and bibliographies can also give you insight into how well the students performed.

Observation.

Decisions are often based on what people observe. Observation is the basis when librarians make such statements as, "since the library instruction program began, the type of reference question has changed," or "students who've taken the library course are often seen helping their friends in the library." While observation techniques can be valuable evaluation tools, they must be carried out systematically if they are to be considered valid.

Common observation techniques include anecdotal records, in which meaningful incidents are written down very soon after they occur; rating scales, in which a set of characteristics or behaviors are rated according to a scale which indicated to what degree they are present; and checklists, which consist of a list of behaviors which are checked off when they occur. Testing textbooks give detailed information on how to develop these tools.

Observation techniques are easy to use in classroom situations, where the students are known and observed over a period of time. Library observations are often difficult. When students are observed in the library, it is usually impossible to know whether or not the student has had instruction. Moreover, what we see is influenced by what we want to see. Reference desks are staffed by a variety of people, some of whom may wish to prove that instruction is beneficial, while other might prefer to demonstrate that it isn't.

Valid observation techniques can be used in the library. A checklist of behavior could be developed and used before an instruction program is developed so that it may serve as a base line for later observation. Students who ask complex reference questions, or who are seen using difficult indexes, can be asked if they have had instruction in library use. It is important to remember, though, that nonsystematic impressions of student behavior are only impressions, subject to many different interpretations.

Surveying Student Opinion and Attitudes

Many times you will be as interested in finding out what students think and feel about your instruction as in how they can perform on a test. Finding out that students enrolled in a library course think it useful, or that the sources covered for the psychology class weren't pertinent to the assigned topics, can be beneficial knowledge. You may also want to know how students reacted to your presentation skills or the materials you used, or whether they thought the activities were worthwhile. So long as the students feel they can be frank and honest (that is, that their answers will not affect their grades), the simplest method is to ask them.

Asking about opinions and attitudes falls within the area of "survey research." Sociologists and market researchers are concerned with survey research, and have written extensively on ways to do it effectively.(9)

> *The world is full of well-meaning people who believe that anyone who can write plain English and has a modicum of common sense can produce a good questionnaire.* (10)

Librarians use questionnaires often, and many times the questionnaires are as hastily conceived and poorly prepared as are locally-produced tests. Following the procedures recommended by survey researchers can help you produce a better product. The same general procedures are used whether you are planning interviews or a questionnaire with written responses.

Steps in developing a survey instrument.

1. Determine what information you want.

While this should be obvious, too many people begin by writing sample questions. You should write down everything you can think of that would be interesting to know. You may decide not to pursue everything, but this way you're assured that you haven't left anything out.

2. Decide upon the method.

Interviews are more commonly used in social research, because of the usual low return of mailed or distributed questionnaires. Interviews, however, are expensive in terms of time. If you can distribute a questionnaire in classes (captive audiences), you will probably get almost a hundred per cent return. If you are sampling your college population, you may choose to interview. (One New York researcher, however, reports that he gets up to an 85% return on questionnaires to college students when they are given a chance on a lottery ticket upon returning the questionnaire.)

3. Choose the form of the questions.

Questions can be either non-structured (open-ended) or structured (fixed responses such as "yes-no" or multiple choice). Open-ended questions allow for freedom of response, but they are time-consuming to score and difficult to categorize. Survey researchers recommend that if you have more than 20 or 30 respondents, you should avoid open-ended questions.

Asking for general comments at the end of the questionnaire lets you solicit the open responses that are sometimes the most interesting part of the questionnaire. Negative comments always seem much more numerous than they actually are. To avoid noticing only these, be careful to count and categorize open responses so that you have a clear idea of what the typical responses are. Some people automatically discard the most positive comment and the most negative one as being nonrepresentative.

4. Determine what background information you need and any"filter" questions necessary.

You will want some demographic information, such as year in school, or major. Filter questions allow you to exclude respondents if you wish. For example, if you are soliciting opinions of how effective your presentation was, one of your first questions should be,"were you present at the library instruction session held for your class?" The responses of those who reply"no" can be set aside.

5. Write questions.

The wording of a question is extremely important. The way a question is worded can elicit conflicting responses. For example, when one national poll asked if "there should be an amendment to the Constitution prohibiting abortions," 38% agreed. A later question in the same poll asked if "there should be an amendment to the Constitution protecting the life of the unborn child;" 50% agreed.(11)

The same problems of ambiguity and lack of clarity that appear in test-item writing also appear in questionnaire-writing. While texts always stress avoiding inexact terms such as"frequently," a common item on library questionnaires is:

> Do you use the library:
>
> A. Frequently. B. Seldom. C. Never.

"Frequently," depending on your point of view, could be anywhere from once a month to once a day. A better version is:

> How often do you use the library in a typical month?
>
> A. Not at all. B. 1 to 3 times. C. 4 or more times.

Questions should also be free of social pressure, since you want students to respond honestly and not the way they think they should. For example, nearly everyone would agree with the statement, "College students should know how to use the library." Different results would probably be obtained with the statement, "College students should have assignments which require the use of the library."

While every text on questionnaire writing has a section on wording, by far the most entertaining (and most referred to) is Payne's *The Art of Asking Questions*. (12)

6. Pretest the questions and revise them.

At the very least, have several of your colleagues read through the questions, looking for poor wording. A better procedure is to administer the questions to several students, having them tell you what they meant by their responses. If a question can be answered in more than one way, it will be.

7. Assemble the questionnaire.

The layout of the questionnaire is important. If it looks crowded or difficult, people will not respond to it. Directions should be clear and brief. Many people refuse to read directions that are more than a sentence long (and some refuse to read directions at all).

If you are mailing a questionnaire, it should be accompanied by a cover letter which explains what you're doing and is convincing enough to entice people to respond. If the questions are to be administered by an interviewer, very complete directions should be written out.

Attitude scales.

If you want to determine what the general attitude of a group of students is towards the library, you will want to use an attitude scale. An attitude scale is made up of a series of statements and yields a single score. The most commonly-used scale, and the easiest to develop, is the Likert-type scale.

A Likert scale typically has up to twenty statements. Here are two sample statements from a library attitude scale:

	SA	agree	neither	disagree	SD
I feel comfortable asking for help in the library	5	4	3	2	1
The library has too many rules and regulations	5	4	3	2	1

Respondents are asked to circle the number which corresponds to their reactions: strongly agree with the statement, agree, neither agree nor disagree,

disagree, strongly disagree.The statements selected should be clearly favorable
or unfavorable. It is also considered important to include both favorable and
unfavorable statements (responses then tend to be more valid), but to avoid
using the word"not." The statements above meet these criteria.

Attitude scales can be used to compare the attitudes of two different groups—
for example, those who have had library instruction and those who have not.
They can be administered twice over a period of time to see if a group has
changed its attitudes—for example, to see if freshmen change their attitudes
by the time they are seniors. Librarians at DePauw University devised an attitude scale that was given before and after instruction to freshmen in both
control and experimental groups. While only a limited change in attitude was
found, both the method and the conclusions are interesting.(13)

Basic texts(14) all give directions on constructing Likert scales, as well as
other scales such as the Thurstone, Guttman, and Osgood scales.

Needs Assessments

A "needs assessment" is a type of survey which asks members of certain
groups to repond with their perception of needs and important goals. For a
library instruction program, the groups to survey would probably be students,
faculty, other librarians, and perhaps administrators. Members of these groups
can be asked to respond to statements in a questionnaire or an interview.

As in the development of any questionnaire or structured interview, you
should start by determining what you want to know. For example, librarians
at SUNY/Oswego wanted to know, among other things, if faculty members
felt that students needed to be able to use a library and if they did indeed learn
how to, and who faculty members thought were the appropriate ones to teach
students library use. With that in mind, these statements, and others, were
developed and distributed. Faculty were asked to indicate if they strongly
agreed, agreed, neither agreed nor disagreed, disagreed, or strongly disagreed
with them:

> In general, students entering college know how to use a library
> effectively.
> As undergraduates at this college, students need to know how to use
> a library effectively.
> Students graduating from this college know how to use a library
> effectively.
> It is the individual student's responsibility to learn how to use the
> library.
> College instructors are the appropriate ones to teach students how
> to use the library.

> *Librarians are the appropriate ones to teach students how to use the*
> *library. (15)*

Needs assessments should be administered before a program is implemented, and the program then developed according to the perceived needs of each key group. However, a needs assessment can be of use at any time, to help you determine if your program is addressing the needs of each group. Finding out that a majority of your faculty members feel that students enter college knowing how to use a library could help you if you are having difficulty setting up course-related instruction. An obvious next step would be to test entering students and publicize the results if they are indeed lacking basic skills.

Measuring Teaching Effectiveness

Since few agree on what the characteristics of a good teacher are, measuring teacher effectiveness is difficult. It is even more difficult in course-related instruction, when you meet with a class only once or twice. Since there is limited time to establish a relationship with students, about all that can be measured are appropriateness of content; usefulness of materials or activities; and presentation skills.

Many texts on speechmaking contain checklists for good delivery techniques.(16) You may wish to ask a colleague to observe one of your classes, or you may want to include questions about your presentation on a student questionnaire. If you do, make sure that the questionnaire is administered soon enough after your presentation that students can remember it.

If you are teaching a library course, there are instruments available which measure teaching effectiveness. Wotruba and Wright (17) examined 21 research studies on teaching effectiveness and described how to develop one's own teacher-rating instrument. Centra (18) describes commercially-available scales as well as discussing the validity of student-rating scales.

Conclusion

There are few data gathering instruments available that bibliographic instruction librarians can use. Most instruments must be locally developed to meet the needs of a particular situation. In order to avoid the faults of most locally-produced instruments, follow these guidelines:

- Decide what information is wanted, being as specific as possible.
- Determine what kind of instrument will yield this information. Make

sure that the instrument is one for which time and resources are available to develop, administer, and score.

• Spend sufficient time in construction. Find out what experts on the particular instrument have to say about how to do it well.

• Have others check the instrument for appropriateness, effectiveness, and good wording. Instead of explaining why a reviewer should have understood what you were trying to say, make changes and appreciate that the problem areas were found before the instrument was actually used for evaluation.

Notes

1. Robert L. Ebel, *Essentials of Educational Measurement*, 2nd ed. (Englewood Cliffs, New Jersey: Prentice-Hall,1971), p.465.

2. Norman E. Gronlund, *Measurement and Evaluation in Teaching*, 4th ed. (New York: Macmillan, 1981), p. 66.

3. Masse Bloomfield, "Testing for Library-Use Competence," in *Educating the Library User*, ed. John Lubans, Jr. (New York: Bowker, 1974), pp. 221-331. The Feagley test is reprinted in Ralph Perkins, *The Prospective Teacher's Knowledge of Library Fundamentals* (Metuchen, NJ: Scarecrow Press, 1965).

4. Representative examples of good textbooks on test construction are Robert L. Ebel, *Essentials of Educational Measurement*, 2d ed. (Englewood Cliffs, NJ: Prentice-Hall, 1971); Norman E. Gronlund, *Measurement and Evaluation of Learning*, 4th ed. (New York: Macmillan, 1981); Arnold J. Lien, *Measurement and Evaluation of Learning*, 4th ed. (Dubuque,Iowa: W. C. Brown, 1980); and William Mehrens and Irving J. Lehman, *Measurement and Evaluation in Education and Psychology* (New York: Holt, 1973).

5. Gronlund, p. 187.

6. Miriam Dudley, *Workbook in Library Skills* (Los Angeles: College Library, University of California Library, 1973).

7. Patricia Knapp, *The Monteith College Library Experiment* (Metuchen, NJ: Scarecrow Press, 1966). Chapter 4 describes the test developed to measure library skills.

8. David N. King and John C. Ory, "Effects of Library Instruction on Student Research: A Case Study," *College and Research Libraries*, 40 (1981), 31-36.

9. Some examples of texts on survey research which discuss the writing of instruments are Charles H. Backstrom, *Survey Research* (Evanston, Ill.: Northwestern University Press, 1963); Abraham N. Oppenheim, *Questionnaire Design and Attitude Measurement* (New York: Basic Books, 1966); and Jeffrey L. Pope, *Practical Marketing Research* (New York: AMACOM, 1981).

10. Oppenheim, p. vii.

11. Pope, p. 59.

12. Stanley L. Payne, *The Art of Asking Questions* (Princeton, NJ: Princeton University Press, 1951).

13. Larry Hardesty, Nicholas P. Lovrich, Jr., and James Mannon, "Evaluating Library-Use Instruction," *College and Research Libraries*, 40 (1981), 309-317.

14. In addition to Oppenheim, see also Marvin Shaw and Jack M. Wright, *Scales for the Measurement of Attitudes*, (New York: McGraw-Hill, 1967), for numerous examples. Volume 5 of Lynn Lyons Morris, et al, *Program Evaluation Kit* (Beverly Hills: Sage, 1978) is a readable discussion of *How to Measure Attitudes*.

15. These statements are taken from an unpublished needs assessment administered to faculty at SUNY/Oswego. Other examples of surveys taken of faculty and students and summaries of their responses can be found in *A Comprehensive Program of User Education for the General Libraries* (Austin, Texas: The University of Texas at Austin General Libraries, 1977),(ERIC ED 148 401).

16. One example is Leon Fletcher, *How to Deliver a Speech* (New York: Chandler, 1973).

17. Thomas R. Wotruba and Penny L. Wright, "How to Develop a Teacher-Rating Instrument," *Journal of Higher Education,* 46 (1975), 653-663.

18. John A. Centra, *Determining Faculty Effectiveness* (San Francisco: Jossey-Bass, 1981).

T. Mark Morey is an Associate Professor of Psychology at the State University of New York at Oswego, with extensive experience in program evaluation. Dr. Morey has recently served as a consultant in the evaluation of the bibliographic instruction program at SUNY/Oswego.

Jacqueline Reihman is an Assistant Professor in the Counseling and Psychological Services Department, State University of New York at Oswego. Dr. Reihman has been involved with the evaluation of human service programs for more than a decade. She and Dr. Morey co-instruct a graduate course in program evaluation.

Chapter Five

Data Management and Statistical Analysis

T. Mark Morey and Jacqueline Reihman

Up to this point the handbook has dealt with a logical sequence of topics which, we hope, has clarified what you would need to do to effectively conduct useful evaluations of your bibliographic instruction programs. Throughout this book we have been trying to convince you that evaluation of bibliographic instruction programs is very important, and that you (perhaps with a little help from your friends) can carry out highly useful and creditable evaluation projects. Simply put, evaluation has been characterized as an effort to provide useful, rational information to facilitate the improvement of bibliographic instruction programs.

There are several aspects to this process. You have to focus clearly on the questions that need asking (through clarification of your goals and objectives), and you need to figure out the best way to ask those questions (through selection and development of tests and measures which reliably ask what you want to ask).

Also, it is important that you conduct your study so that the answers to your original questions can be reasonably well understood and explained (through research designs and sample selection which assist in comparing competing explanations for your results). An additional component is needed, however, before you would actually have evaluative results which could be discussed and presented to others or used as a basis for decisions about your program: the component of data management and statistical analysis. These areas concern procedures needed to describe, refine, verify, and effectively use the information which you obtained in your evaluation study. Without the "language" of statistics you would be unable to interpret and communicate the results of your evaluation study. That is, you need to use these tools to answer the questions that stimulated your evaluation effort in the first place.

While the content in this chapter follows logically in the sequence of the handbook, it will soon become apparent to you that knowledge of data management and statistics is helpful in the early planning of an evaluation study. For example, knowing that you have the availability of machine scoring and computer analysis for your study may directly influence such things as item selection, formatting of instruments, and subject selection. Also, knowing that you have the facilities for doing rather sophisticated statistical techniques may help you to decide upon your research design. Nonetheless, often it is only after you have gathered a batch of information from an evaluation study that you become convinced how necessary it is to know something about data management and statistical analysis.

This chapter is intended to address three general goals. The first is to convince you that data management and statistical analysis are useful, important, and non-mystical tools that are essential to effective evaluation. Second, after reading the chapter you should be confident that, given typically available resources, you can make effective use of even highly sophisticated statistical procedures without straining your mathematical or conceptual capabilities. Third, the chapter should provide you with an introduction to these areas by emphasizing a straightforward understanding of some of the most important concepts and a pragmatic approach to finding necessary resources. We hope that you will see that a librarian does not have to become a mathematician, computer scientist, or statistician to use competently and confidently the appropriate techniques of data management and analysis. You can find the answers to your evaluative questions and explore the "thrill" of statistical significance, without devoting your life to the study of quantitative analysis.

Before going any further, let's deal with two general questions that will be more completely answered as the chapter progresses. The first question is, "what can data management and statistical analysis do for me?" And the second question is, "what knowledge and resources do I need to do an effective job in these areas?"

When you collect a batch of information for an evaluation study, a number of needs will undoubtedly emerge. For example, you would commonly have the need to:

    a. deal with a large amount of information quickly and easily;
    b. summarize findings so that the evaluation questions can be dealt with more simply;
    c. present the findings to others in ways that are generally acceptable, understood, and economical;
    d. know whether the measurement devices of the individual questionnaire items that you used are reliable and useful;
    e. seek help in making decisions regarding what the results of the study mean relative to the evaluation questions you originally asked (e.g., "did the instruction actually increase the students' ability to plan an efficient research strategy?");
    f. explore or test for important relationships between and among variables that affect the quality of your bibliographic instruction program.

All of these needs are directly addressed by the concepts introduced in this chapter.

Specific answers to the question about what is actually needed to be effective in analyzing data varies from situation to situation. However, nearly every evaluation project will involve the following tasks:

    a. gathering and recording information,
    b. compiling and collating information,
    c. choosing appropriate statistical procedures and analyses,
    d. performing the analyses,
    e. recording and tabulating results, and
    f. interpreting the findings.

As has been suggested, on most college campuses you will be able to find experts who would be ready, willing and able to assist you in completing some or all of these tasks. With regard to statistical analysis, it is particularly helpful to find someone who is knowledgeable about statistics and skillful in the use of computers. Again, it is likely that you would find statistical and computer experts in disciplines such as the social sciences, mathematics, or computer science. Specifically, you might want to find individuals who teach courses in research design, program evaluation, or statistics. One important point to remember is that your experts should be consulted early in the planning of your project so they can help in making important decisions as your project takes form. Early consultation avoids the all-too-common pitfall of collecting a set of data which are difficult or impossible to analyze properly. A skilled collaborator could easily be your most important resource in carrying out a successful evaluation project. It is well worth any additional time (and possibly money) this may cost you. If successful in finding help, your main task may be to communicate what you intend to do and how the collaborator can help you.

Even if you have had the good fortune to locate someone to do "all" of the data management and statistics for you, you will still have to know something about these areas. You will be able to work more effectively with your colleagues if you have a general grasp of fundamental concepts and procedures involved. Of course, the more you have to do yourself, the more you will have to know. Happily, there are a variety of textbooks and handbooks which can take you from the most elementary understanding of statistics to the highest level of sophistication necessary. The remainder of this chapter will assist your understanding of the central concepts involved in data management and statistics. However, you will want to consult the chapter bibliography for a sample of texts you might find useful. For example, excellent discussions of introductory statistics are found in Weinberg and Schumaker's book (1) and the text written by Welkowitz, et. al.(2) For assistance in computing statistics, you might like to use the handbook by Bruning and Kintz.(3) And for a concise summary of the areas of data management and statistics, as well as information on how to use a computer to best advantage, you would want to consult the manuals which accompany the Statistical Package for the Social Sciences (SPSS).(4)

Second only to the human resources which we mentioned earlier, computers and easy-to-use computer programs for data analysis can be your most important resource. While it is entirely possible for you to do all of the data management and statistics for an evaluation study by hand (or by using an inexpensive calculator), computers are more efficient. The SPSS software package mentioned earlier is easy to use, complete, and available on most college campuses. A statistical package (such as SPSS) allows anyone who can spend a few hours reading a manual to perform complex statistical procedures easily which would otherwise require a considerable amount of skill and time. Additionally, not only can these procedures be performed very quickly by a computer, but the printouts are fashioned in a format that can be easily communicated to others. We will continue to reference SPSS subprograms in the remainder of this chapter. However, since there are other good statistical packages available, you should check on your own campus which computer resources are accessible and appropriate for your use.

A Case Example

To illustrate the central concepts more clearly, we'd like for you to imagine that you have just finished collecting data for a small-scale evaluation study of a bibliographic instruction program. You are evaluating a freshman-level bibliographic instruction program designed to develop the library research skills of students who are enrolled in an advanced composition course. The bibliographic instruction is offered once each quarter with about 15 students enrolled in each half of the semester. Given the goals and objectives of the instruction program, you have decided to obtain several different types of information from the students. You have developed two forms of a short 20-item Library Skills Test (LST) designed to assess the students' competence. With the help of your colleagues, you have worked on the development of the LST, and performed some routine, but very useful, analyses on the LST itself to assess its reliability and validity. Your college, as is true of most, made that job rather easy for you by providing computer scoring and item analysis which allowed you to judge which items best discriminate among student performances. Besides the LST you have decided to obtain some descriptive background data about the students and also to ask for their opinions about the instruction.

Before the evaluation study began, you had chosen items and worked to develop three measurement instruments, the LST (a 20-item fixed-choice, machine-scorable test), a Background Survey (a four-item questionnaire which seeks information about the students and the student's previous library experience), and a very short Program Questionnaire (a three-item instrument requesting their views of the instruction). The Background Survey asks for the following information:

a. gender;
b. high school average (GPA);
c. size of high school student body; and
d. typical amount of previous library use.

The Program Questionnaire addresses the following three pieces of information:

a. a rating of the student's competence in making effective use of the library;
b. a rating of the library instructor; and
c. whether the student would recommend the program for other classes.

For ease in scoring, all of the items on the Background Survey and the Program Questionnaire were put into a forced-choice format (i.e., the student must choose one of the options offered for each item).

Further imagine that you chose to use a true experimental design, one which allowed you to feel confident that your study would assess the impact of your program. Thirty students who were enrolled in the composition course during the semester were randomly divided into two groups of 15 each. One group was assigned to the bibliographic instruction program in the first quarter (the experimental group) while the control group was to take it the second quarter. All 30 of the students were given one form of the LST and the Background Survey at the beginning of the semester. At the end of the first quarter, both groups of students were given an alternate form of the LST, and the experimental group completed the Program Questionnaire. By that point in the semester you had essentially completed a true pretest, post-test experimental design, with random assignment of subjects and tests administered both before and after the course intervention. The students who had been in the control group, however, had the opportunity to attend the bibliographic instruction sessions during the second quarter. Subsequently, you had them take the LST again and complete the Program Questionnaire at the end of the semester. That provided you with additional information to complete your evaluation study. We will refer to that LST score as the post-post-test.

Even with our hypothetical study, which is limited in scope, the completion of the data-collection phase always results in a sizeable array of information for each subject who participated. Specifically, in our study, there would be Background Survey responses, several sets of LST scores and responses to the Program Questionnaire for each of 30 persons.

At this point, there is a clear need to organize these pieces of information into some manageable form. Unless all of the information can be put together in one place, you would have to shuffle through all of your tests, surveys and questionnaires several times while trying to answer your various evaluation questions. The easiest and most straightforward method of doing this is to create a data management matrix (see following page). This will mean that you will collate all of the information you have collected in one large array with each piece of information having one specific location. Although this sounds complicated, it is really quite simple. The general idea is to create a matrix in which the rows contain information about each subject and the columns contain data for each category of information. To illustrate this, we have constructed a data management matrix for our hypothetical study. Each cell of the matrix contains a number, which represents either an actual obtained value (e.g., high school average) or a number used as a code for some categorical designation (e.g., for gender, $1 =$ males, and $2 =$ females). Whether this matrix is done on paper or put into a computer file, it will allow you to be much more efficient in combining and analyzing the file.

Subject	1-Group Designation: 1=exp. 2=unexp.	2-Gender: 1=male 2=female	3-High School Average	4-High School Size (1-5)	5-Previous Library Use (1-3)	6-LST pre-test (0-20)	7-LST post-test (0-20)	8-LST post post-test (0-20)	9-Competence (1-3)	10-Instructor (1-4)	11-Recommend Program (1-4)
S1	1	2	82	1	1	8	15		2	3	3
S2	2	2	87	5	3	9	10	14	3	3	3
S3	1	1	91	3	2	9	15		2	3	2
S4	2	2	84	2	1	8	8	16	1	4	3
S5	1	2	82	2	2	6	18		3	3	4
S6	2	2	89	4	3	7	5	15	2	4	3
S7	1	1	91	3	1	11	19		1	4	4
S8	2	2	92	1	2	10	10	19	1	4	4
S9	1	1	87	4	3	7	13		3	3	2
S10	2	2	83	1	1	7	6	17	1	4	4
S11	1	2	90	3	2	8	13		2	4	4
S12	2	1	96	3	2	9	9	15	2	4	4
S13	1	2	81	2	2	5	14		3	4	3
S14	2	2	83	3	1	8	7	13	1	3	2
S15	1	1	85	3	3	7	17		2	3	1
S16	2	2	85	3	3	7	9	16	3	4	4
S17	1	1	89	3	3	6	16		3	4	4
S18	2	2	90	2	1	8	7	16	1	4	4
S19	1	2	92	4	2	11	16		1	4	3
S20	2	2	87	3	3	7	7	18	3	4	3
S21	1	1	86	2	1	5	16		1	3	3
S22	2	1	84	3	3	8	8	14	3	3	3
S23	1	2	88	3	2	10	20		1	3	2
S24	2	2	88	2	1	8	7	15	1	3	3
S25	1	1	89	3	3	9	18		3	3	3
S26	2	2	94	3	3	7	9	16	2	3	2
S27	1	2	91	3	3	8	16		1	3	4
S28	2	1	89	2	1	6	6	14	3	4	4
S29	1	1	88	3	2	8	17		3	4	4
S30	2	1	93	3	2	10	6	15	2	4	4

Introduction to Statistical Analyses

Descriptive Measures

After you have successfully constructed a data management matrix, you will probably want to describe and summarize the information in each of the columns. It is always a good idea to begin your statistical analysis with this descriptive step. Not only do you obtain extremely useful information during this summarizing process, but you will become more familiar with your data. This process will also enable you to detect any errors you might have made either in coding your data or in data entry.

The typical kinds of descriptive and summary statistics used in evaluation include measures of **central tendency** and measures of **dispersion** or **variability.** Simply stated, central tendency refers to average scores and dispersion refers to how tightly the array of scores are clustered together (e.g., the high school averages range from 81 to 96).

Although all measures of central tendency (i.e., mean, median and mode) are useful in certain circumstances, we will focus here on the **mean.** The definition of a mean is probably familiar to you—it is simply an arithmetic average. Several measures of dispersion exist (e.g., range, variance, and standard deviation). However, dispersion is most commonly indexed by **standard deviation** which provides a measure of average deviation or average spread of scores around the mean of a distribution of scores. An example here might clarify things. Question B on the Background Survey asked students: "What was your high school average?" If you wanted to describe high school averages, you could go to the appropriate column (3) of your data management matrix and calculate an arithmetic average, or mean, of those scores:

$$S_1 = 82; S_2 = 87; S_3 = 91 \ldots S_{30} = 93.$$

The mean of this array is 87.87 and the standard deviation is 3.82. This amount of variability is really quite large; contrast this to a hypothetical situation in which all 30 students have averages between 85 and 88. The mean of this hypothetical array might also be 87.87, but the standard deviation would be much smaller. It should be clear to you that although the mean, or average score, is precisely the same for both distributions, the standard deviation differs markedly. In the first group, the high school averages are much more spread out than they are in the second group. To describe a distribution of scores fully, both measures of central tendency and dispersion are necessary since reporting only one could lead to possible misinterpretation.

Sometimes, however, you will have data which are not meaningfully described by means and standard deviations. Our classification of gender is a good example. Since there were 18 females (coded as two) and 12 males (coded as one) in our study, we could calculate a mean of the code numbers, which would be 1.60 and a standard deviation, which is .50. However, as you can see, this doesn't really make sense. In cases like this one, where the numbers reflect different categories of information, it is much more meaningful and appropriate to present summaries in percentages or frequencies. These kinds of data are referred to as "categorical data." If we reevaluate our gender example now, we can see that it makes intuitive (as well as statistical) sense to report that, "Of 30 subjects in our study, 60 percent are female and 40 percent are male."

What if we had more than two categories of information—what would be the best way to report a summary of that variable? The answer is easy—simply extend the logic described in the gender example. Question C of the Background Survey asked students to indicate the size of the high school they attended. Students were asked to respond in one of the following categories: 0-500=1; 501-1000=2; 1001-1500=3; 1501-2000=4; or greater than 2000=5. Percentages can be calculated easily for these data:

Size Category	Number Respondents	Percent Total
0 - 500	3	10
501 - 1,000	7	23
1,001 - 1,500	16	53
1,501 - 2,000	3	10
► - 2,000	1	3

(A point to remember is that when you report percentages, you should *always* include the total number on which the percentages are based.) However, one picture can be worth a thousand words. This is particularly true when you are presenting categorical information. It is an excellent idea to provide graphic representation. This is easily done with a **histogram,** which is a type of bar graph. Our data on high school size could be represented in the manner shown on the following page. Often even those who claim a disdain for statistics can easily grasp information presented graphically.

Fortunately, many computer software packages will provide descriptive information for you. In SPSS, the subprogram CONDESCRIPTIVE is appropriate if you are interested in describing your data with means and standard deviations. If your data are categorical in nature, the SPSS subprogram FREQUENCIES will generate frequencies, percentages, and even histograms.

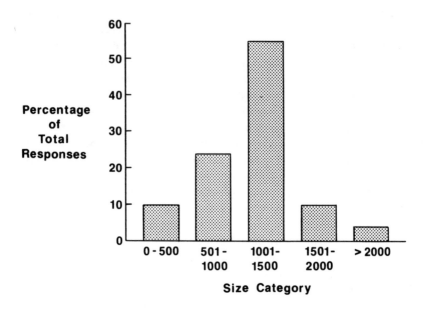

Differences Between Groups

Once you have fully described the data, it is time to respond to your original evaluation questions. This relates directly to the design you chose at the beginning of your study. The principal evaluative question for our case example is, "Do people who have had the bibliographic instruction have higher LST scores than those people who have not had the instruction?"

Quite clearly, this question concerns differences between groups, specifically differences between the experimental group which received the instruction and the control group which did not. In particular, we need to compare the post-treatment scores of the experimental group with the post-treatment scores of the control group. This kind of comparison would be done with something called an **independent samples t-test.** The t-test is an **inferential statistic** designed to evaluate the mean differences between two independent (not related) groups. These differences are compared statistically and evaluated as to whether the obtained differences (between the two groups means) were likely to have occurred by change alone. It is important to remember that it is generally very unlikely that two randomly-created groups will have exactly the same mean for almost any variable (consider weight, for example). We need to see if our obtained difference is "real" or due to chance. In our example, we are comparing experimental and control scores located in column seven of the data management matrix. The experimental group's mean score on the post-treatment LST was 16.2 and the control group's score on the same measure was 7.6. After calculating the "t" value for this comparison we would use a table in a statistics book to find that the value of "t" indicates that our difference was statistically significant. The probability that the obtained difference was due to chance was less than .01 (or less than one in one hundred). We would be able to respond confidently to our original question and conclude that, "Yes, the instruction does result in students' having higher LST scores."

Having demonstrated that the treatment was effective in producing higher scores on the LST, you might then ask, "How much change occurred as a function of the bibliographic instruction?" Once again, your interest would focus on differences between groups of scores. This time, however, the comparison of interest is between the experimental group's pre-treatment and post-treatment scores (look at columns six and seven in the matrix for experimental subjects). In this case, though, since your groups are related (in fact, they are each individual's measurements at two different times), you would perform something called a **paired-samples t-test**. This version of the t-test adjusts for the fact that individuals' scores before treatment are systematically related to their scores after treatment. After performing the t-test, we would find that the pre-treatment scores for the experimental group (mean of 7.87) differed significantly from their post-treatment scores (mean of 16.20). Not only is this a statistically significant difference, but you would be able to say that students having bibliographic instruction would typically have their LST scores raised about seven points. SPSS has a fine discussion of these two kinds of t-tests and has the capability of computing either of them for you in the subprogram T-TEST.

You may be wondering what would happen if you had more than two groups in your experimental design. Not surprisingly, the logic of the t-test is extended to any number of groups you might have. Instead of comparing mean differences for only two groups, mean differences among several groups may be compared simultaneously. The statistical procedure appropriate to this kind of situation is called an **Analysis of Variance (ANOVA)**. We will not be concerned with this technique in the present chapter. The interested reader is referred to the listing at the end of this chapter.

Relationships Between Variables

Often, your interest will be in examining relationships which might exist between variables rather than in differences between groups. You might want to know, for example, if high school grade point average is systematically related to pre-treatment LST scores. In other words, do students with high averages in high school tend also to have high scores on the LST and, conversely, do students with low averages have low LST scores?

A statistical technique designed to assess the magnitude and strength of a relationship between two or more variables is called the **Pearson Product Moment Correlation.** This technique not only allows one to measure the strength of the relationship, but the type of relationship as well (i.e., direct or inverse). For a perfect direct relationship, the correlation coefficient "r" equals $+1.0$ and a perfect inverse relationship results in an "r" of -1.0.

In our case example we have a direct (or positive) relationship between high school average and pre-treatment LST scores. This relationship is reflected in the obtained correlation value, $+.53$. One of the easiest ways to visualize the relationship between two variables is to construct a scattergram. A scattergram is a two-dimensional plot of the intersection of individual's scores on each of the two different variables. A scattergram of the intersection of these scores for our example would be constructed as shown below:

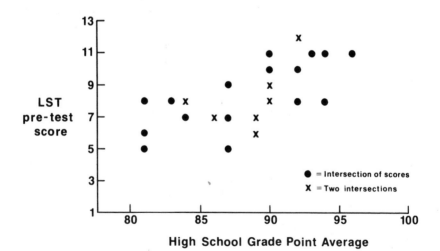

A pattern has emerged: if you drew a line around the perimeter of the intersections, you would have an ellipse which slanted upward from left to right. As high school average increases, so do LST scores, which reflects the positive relationship we found. On the other hand, if test scores increased while high school averages decreased (an unlikely possibility), the obtained relationship would have been negative. Of course, it is altogether possible that two variables might not be related in any systematic fashion. If that were the case, no discernible pattern would emerge in the scattergram (i.e., no oblong form or slant would be seen) and the correlation would be close to zero.

Correlational procedures are very useful in exploring whether variables are systematically related to one another. However, some caveats exist in interpreting correlational results. Correlations simply indicate association—they do not indicate cause-and-effect. In other words, from correlational findings, it is not possible to draw conclusions whether either of the variables caused the other. Variables are often found to be related without one causing the other. Teams often have "home" and "away" uniforms, but it is silly to insist that a "home" winning streak and an "away" losing streak are due to the color of the uniform. In our example, we may accurately state that high school grade point average is positively related to pre-treatment LST scores. It is not possible to conclude that high school averages caused LST scores to occur as they did.

Correlational methods are closely aligned with another very useful technique used in evaluation. Multiple regression techniques allow the evaluator to use a number of variables (independent) to predict one other variable (dependent). If interest in the present evaluative study had focused on "prediction" of post-treatment LST scores rather than on evaluating the success of the library instruction in increasing LST scores, you might have collected additional information you thought might be related to LST performance. An example might be SAT verbal scores. Multiple regression is the precise procedure that would allow you to measure the combined relationships of high school average and SAT verbal scores in predicting LST scores.

Fortunately, SPSS again has subprograms available for obtaining both correlation and regression analyses. Subprogram **PEARSON CORR** calculates the correlation coefficient and plots two-dimensional scattergrams and subprogram **REGRESSION** will compute regression analyses.

Finally, you might want to assess relationships which exist between categorical variables. Categorical data represent information which is indexed by mutually exclusive categories. For instance, question D on the Background Survey asked students to indicate their typical amount of previous library use. They were asked to respond with one of the following categories:

    a. 0-1 times a month (equals 1);
    b. 2-4 times a month (equals 2);
    c. more than 4 times a month (equals 3).

You might think that frequency of library use is related to one's sense of confidence in library skills. Question A of the Program Questionnaire asks students to rate their sense of competence using the following categories:

    a. little or no confidence (equals 1);
    b. a fair amount of confidence (equals 2); or
    c. a great deal of confidence (equals 3).

These two variables are found in columns 5 and 9, respectively, of the data management matrix. If you wanted to assess the relationship between these variables, the appropriate technique to use is called a **Chi-Square Test of Association.** You construct a twofold table and note the frequencies that occur in each cell, as shown below:

Frequency of Use

		0-1/month	2-4/month	>4/month
	little amount	7	1	1
Sense of Competence	fair amount	3	4	3
	great deal	1	3	7

These frequencies which have occurred are compared to frequencies which would occur if the two variables were not at all related to each other (i.e., were independent of each other). A statistically significant chi-square value indicates that a relationship exists. Chi-square tests are particularly useful in evaluations where a great deal of the information collected is categorical in nature. SPSS has a subprogram which calculates chi-square values (subprogram CONTINGENCY).

While there are many other specific statistical procedures, the examples which we have used in this chapter have presented the core concepts upon which all statistical procedures are based. While varying in complexity, all statistical procedures are intended to summarize and describe, test for differences between groups of values, or clarify and define relationships between variables. Without minimizing all of the many things that you can go on to learn about statistics we do hope that this brief introduction has given you a confident grasp of the main themes you will find (played in variations) as you continue to learn more about the realm of statistical analysis.

Conclusion

We hope that this chapter has further convinced you that effective data management and statistical analysis are essential components of evaluation, and that you can competently use these tools to assist you in evaluating your bibliographic instruction programs. At this point you should have a sense of what these tools might do for you, and a clear idea of the resources you might draw upon to assist you. Helpful experts, computers and statistical packages, and well-written texts on statistics should greatly facilitate the accomplishment of your evaluation goals. A broad conceptual understanding of data management and analysis will serve you well in making further use of the resources which are available to you, and will provide you with a basis for your use of these concepts and procedures in the evaluation of your programs.

Suggested Reading

See Bibliography for full entry.

Hays (1981)
Helwig (1979)
Runyon (1976)
Spatz (1976)

Notes

1. G. H. Weinberg and J. A. Schumaker, *Statistics: An Intuitive Approach,* 3d ed. (Monterey, Calif.: Brooks/Cole, 1974).

2. J. Welkowitz, R. B. Ewen, and I. Cohen, *Introductory Statistics for the Behavioral Sciences,* 3d ed. (New York: Academic Press, 1982).

3. J. L. Bruning and B. L. Kintz, *Computational Handbook of Statistics,* 2nd ed. (Glenview, Ill.: Scott Foresman, 1977). Good for examples and for working with a calculator.

4. N. Nie, *SPSS, Combined Edition* (New York: McGraw-Hill, 1981). Contains complete documentation for a good statistical package for computers.

Richard Hume Werking is Associate Director for Collection Development and Assistant Professor of History at Trinity University in San Antonio. His research interests include library collections and services, and he has presented or published several papers on aspects of bibliographic education.

Chapter Six

Significant Works

Richard Hume Werking

Some of the pieces summarized here are more significant than others. Moreover, none of the studies is without its flaws, and hence inclusion in this chapter should not be construed as an "endorsement" by me or by the subcommittee responsible for producing this manual. At the same time, I do consider these works the best of the lot as representatives of their particular genre and selected them on that basis.

Hopefully, the summaries constitute an aggregation that will prove useful for librarians interested in learning more about evaluating bibliographic education, and perhaps about evaluating other things as well. For a more extensive introduction to the literature, I refer readers to my review article, "Evaluating Bibliographic Education: A Review and Critique," described below.

James Benson. "Bibliographic Education: A Radical Assessment."In *Proceedings from the Second Southeastern Conference on Approaches to Bibliographic Instruction.* Ed. Cerise Oberman-Soroka. Charleston, South Carolina: College of Charleston, 1980, pp. 53-68.

In what is one of the most important pieces in the field of bibliographic education (and probably the most ignored), a skeptic looks at that subject and in the process raises some important questions about evaluation. Benson scoffs at anecdotal evidence gathered from students as a means of evaluating the effectiveness of instruction, and he demands instead "proof" that takes the form of "aggregate statistical data." More useful are his thoughtfulness about the problems associated with evaluation and his emphasis on distinguishing between a presumed ability to use libraries and the actual use of libraries. "The point is, simply, that evaluation of bibliographic instruction must be based on usage outcomes rather than skills."

Masse Bloomfield. "Testing for Library-Use Competence." In *Educating the Library User.* Ed. John Lubans, Jr. New York: Bowker, 1974, pp. 221-231.

Bloomfield's chapter analyzes sixteen library-use tests. He devotes much of his attention to the most popular such test, Edith M. Feagley, et al., *A Library Orientation Test for College Freshmen* (Teachers College, Columbia University, 1955). Bloomfield gives numerous examples of, and also raises questions about, these tests. The chapter concludes with a bibliography of tests.

Susan Burton. "Objective Tests as an Evaluation Tool: Problems in Construction and Use." In *Library Instruction in the Seventies: State of the Art.* Ed. Hannelore Rader. Ann Arbor, MI: Pieran Press, 1977, pp. 99-103.

At the Undergraduate Library of the University of Texas at Austin, librarians found that sometimes evaluation does not necessarily provide answers but instead may just raise additional questions. Burton here summarizes the advantages and disadvantages of objective tests, placing them within the context of a bibliographic instruction program. She also provides a useful, albeit brief, look at how a group of instruction librarians were prompted to reconsider their assumptions, not only about evaluation *per se,* but about other aspects of the instruction program as well. She concludes that objective tests are one important evaluation tool for instruction librarians, and that they "are practically guaranteed to make us face up to whatever assumptions we have about what students know, don't know, or should know about finding information in libraries."

Nancy Fjallbrant. "Evaluation in a User Education Programme." *Journal of Librarianship* 9 (April 1977), 83-95.

The article discusses the purposes of evaluation, following with a brief and good description of the concepts, scope, methods, and timing of evaluation. Examples of previous evaluation of library user instruction are given. The final part of the article is an account of the evaluation work carried out in connection with the development of a user education program at the Chalmers

University of Technology Library, Gothenburg, Sweden. Fjallbrant describes the evaluation methods used in her program. Her article is another good example of the generally more eclectic approach to evaluation followed by instruction librarians in Britain (or, like Fjallbrant, trained in Britain) compared with most of their American counterparts.

Larry Hardesty, Nicholas P. Lovrich, Jr., and James Mannon. "Evaluating Library-Use Instruction." *College and Research Libraries* 40 (1979), 309-317.

Using control and experimental groups, together with pre-and post-testing, the investigators found that the students at DePauw University receiving instruction scored significantly higher than those in the control group on a 20-item test. The test asked students to indicate which area of the library was "the most logical place to start" a search for information such as census data, a magazine article or a particular book. The authors also measured the change in certain student attitudes before and after instruction, concluding that such change was much harder to effect than changes in library use skills. The product of collaboration among a librarian, a political scientist, and a sociologist, this article serves as the most explicit example to date of evaluation undertaken to justify bibliographic education to college and university administrators. For additional discussion of the strengths and weaknesses of the article, see Werking (1980), cited below.

Colin Harris. "Illuminative Evaluation of User Education Programmes." *ASLIB Proceedings* 29 (October 1977), 348-362.

The author describes the development of an illuminative evaluation strategy in a user education project, the Travelling Workshops Experiment based at Newcastle upon Tyne Polytechnic Library. The classic social science research model was considered inappropriate for the experiment, and the project staff turned to the less formal and relatively "goal free" method known as "illuminative evaluation." That approach is an eclectic one, including a variety of methods: observation, interviews, questionnaires, and tests, among others. It aims

> to study the innovatory project: how it operates; how it is influenced by the various school situations in which it is applied; what those directly concerned regard as its advantages and disadvantages; and how students' intellectual tasks and academic experiences are most affected. . . In short, it seeks to address and to illuminate a complex array of questions.

Harris concludes that neither librarians nor others will develop the tools "to **measure** precisely the contributions of such a variety of factors to the success of a programme," and that it is more important "to be aware of the potential influence of all factors and to be able to make informed guesses about their contributions."

> David N. King and John C. Ory. "Effects of Library Instruction on Student Research: A Case Study." *College and Research Libraries* 42 (1981), 31-41.

Among the more important evaluation studies in recent years, this is one of a handful that focus on student use of library services and resources. King and Ory administered a questionnaire to three groups of freshmen at the University of Illinois: those who had received instruction from librarians; those who had received rather similar instruction from a teaching assistant; and those who had received no instruction. Students were asked how many reference and information sources they had used while researching their term papers. Not surprisingly, students who had received instruction were found to have used a greater variety of sources and seemed to have more confidence in their ability to use the library. Although not noted by the authors, the data seem to indicate that students instructed by the teaching assistant performed their research as creditably as those instructed by librarians.

The strength of the study lies in its description of information-gathering techniques, as well as the authors' recognition of the importance of gauging library use.

> Thomas G. Kirk. "A Comparison of Two Methods of Library Instruction for Students in Introductory Biology." *College and Research Libraries* 32 (1971), 465-74.

This article is important neither because of its most explicit focus, the comparison of two methods of bibliographic instruction, nor its finding that neither method proved superior. That focus and finding are both commonplace in educational research, although they were not so well-known in bibliographic instruction when Kirk's article was published. Rather, the significance of this study lies in Kirk's sensible combination of high quality bibliographic instruction with quantitative analysis of some **products** of instructional efforts—the students' library papers and their bibliographies. Together with Knapp's work, cited below, his account should serve as a model for future efforts to design as well as to evaluate user education.

Thomas G. Kirk. "Evaluation of Library Orientation and Instruction Programs:A Taxonomy." In *Planning and Developing a Library Instruction Program.* Ed. Mary Bolner. Ann Arbor, MI: Pieran Press, 1975, pp. 41-51.

Kirk's "taxonomy" of evaluation is an extremely useful overview, especially for librarians new to the subject. It discusses several kinds of informal and formal evaluation, and it helpfully distinguishes among four kinds of formal evaluation: of the instruction's **content,** of its **product,** of the **process** of library use, and of **attitudes.**

Patricia B. Knapp. *The Montieth College Library Experiment.* Metuchen, NJ: Scarecrow Press, 1966. Especially Chapter IV and Appendix I.

Knapp's classic study is frequently cited; yet its contents are ignored even by many of those who cite the title. Unlike virtually every other published study of evaluation in bibliographic education, Knapp attempted to analyze, define, and measure library competence by studying library use. Her book usefully details the variety and interplay of different evaluation methods undertaken during the course of the Montieth experiment.

Penelope Pearson and Virginia Tiefel. "Evaluating Undergraduate Library Instruction at the Ohio State University." *Journal of Academic Librarianship* 7 (1982), 351-357.

Pearson and Tiefel report on several evaluations of the program to teach very basic "library skills" to freshmen at Ohio State University. Using a questionnaire, librarians gathered from students information about their previous library instruction, their opinions about the instruction they were receiving and their suggestions for improving it, their attitudes toward libraries. At the same time they tested the students for information retention. One interesting aspect of the evaluations was a telephone poll of students conducted by an independent survey organization. The article's strength lies in its straightforward discussion of how the evaluations were conducted.

Shelley Phipps and Ruth Dickstein. "The Library Skills Program at the University of Arizona: Testing, Evaluation, and Critique." *Journal of Academic Librarianship* 5 (September 1979), 205-214.

Phipps and Dickstein studied the effectiveness of the library's workbook in meeting instructional goals by means of pre- and post-testing. The principal strength of this article is that it provides an analysis and observations for each question on the test, demonstrating which portions of the exam achieved their objectives and which did not. Also, the authors candidly and helpfully note several problems with the experiment.

Barbara A. Schwartz and Susan Burton. *Teaching Library Skills in Freshman English: An Undergraduate Library's Experience.* Austin, Texas: The University of Texas at Austin, 1981. Chapter VI, "Evaluation."

Schwartz and Burton devote a chapter of this detailed program description to an account of their experience with evaluation, which serves also as a close look at some of evaluation's problems and prospects. After spending a great deal of time and energy attempting to develop a satisfactory objective test, the librarians at the University of Texas Undergraduate Library scrapped that effort and turned to questionnaires as a better tool for their purposes, including the measurement of long-term impact. In 1978 they administered to students a questionnaire and compared the responses with those to a similar survey undertaken in 1975. (Although distributed and collected by different methods, the response rate to both surveys was 47 percent.) Students responded to specific questions about their purposes for using the library and their methods of using library resources for papers or research projects. The results of the 1978 survey indicated to the librarians that their instructional program had "made a significant and lasting impact on students' reported library behavior." One especially interesting discovery made by the librarians was that, once the instruction program was under way, the faculty and administration accepted it as part of the freshman English curriculum and were much less concerned than the librarians about evaluating in order to obtain hard data.

Thomas T. Surprenant. "Learning Theory, Lecture, and Programmed Instruction Text: An Experiment in Bibliographic Instruction." *College and Research Libraries* 43 (1982), 31-37.

The author conducted this experiment at several colleges in northern Minnesota and Michigan. Using the classical "botanical" approach, with pretesting, post-testing, hypotheses, and control groups, Surprenant found not only that students receiving basic bibliographic instruction performed significantly better on a paper-and-pencil test than those with no instruction, but also that students receiving programmed instruction performed significantly better than students who received a lecture. He also distinguishes between "factual" and "application" questions, finding programmed instruction giving superior results for both kinds. A considerable portion of the article is a plea for greater use of programmed instruction, and the piece concludes with the almost inevitable call for more research.

The article's principal strength lies in Surprenant's careful delineation of the steps necessary for this approach, and his use of a clear and straightforward prose style. Unfortunately, the test is not reproduced with the article, a common but still undesirable characteristic, especially since readers would likely be interested in the categorization of "factual" and "application" questions.

There is no indication that the author pursued two of the more interesting possibilities for investigation: differences in variance among the groups, and differences in effectiveness among the four librarians who lectured to the students.

Richard Hume Werking. "Evaluating Bibliographic Education: A Review and Critique." *Library Trends* 29 (Summer 1980), 153-172.

This essay provides a relatively recent overview of the literature dealing with the evaluation of bibliographic education. The author discusses problems inherent in evaluation, and he raises questions about what constitutes proof of success.

Richard Hume Werking. *Lawrence University's Library Service Enhancement Program: A Report on the Planning Year (1977).* Bethseda, MD: Educational Resources Information Center, 1977. (ED 144 576). Especially pp. 3ff, Appendix C.

A small portion of this report describes a survey of 142 students, randomly selected from among a student population of about 1300. The survey, intended chiefly as a needs assessment, provided helpful information about what the students did in the library, what they knew about library research materials, and what they thought about their library activities; it obtained a response rate of 94 percent. The logistics of conducting the survey are described in considerable detail.

Marvin E. Wiggins. "The Development of Library Use Instructional Programs." *College and Research Libraries* 33 (1972), 473-479.

Several units of programmed instruction were developed at the Brigham Young University Library to teach the student body basic library skills. Each program defined behavioral objectives (both terminal and enabling) and matched objectives with test questions. Then instruction consistent with the test and behavioral objectives was written. Students were pretested before receiving either programmed or nonprogrammed instruction; some pretested students received no instruction. Wiggins found that the scores of students receiving either programmed or nonprogrammed instruction showed statistically significant improvement on the post-test over the scores of students in the control group.

One potential problem with the study was that post-testing apparently was done immediately following instruction, since one of its purposes was to provide a reinforcement of learning.

John Mark Tucker is Senior Reference Librarian at Purdue University. As Reference Librarian at Wabash College, he worked with the College Library Program, funded by the Council on Library Resources and designed to further integrate the use of the library into undergraduate education. He has written several articles on the history of bibliographic instruction.

Glossary

John Mark Tucker

This glossary is a highly selective list of terms drawn from nomenclature currently used in research and evaluation in the field of education. The definitions are intended to be as jargon-free and yet as accurate as possible. Entries were adapted from the following sources: Busha, Charles H., and Stephen P. Harter, *Research Methods in Librarianship; Techniques and Interpretation* (New York: Teachers College Press, Columbia University, 1977); *The Encyclopedia of Education* (New York: Macmillan and Free Press, 1971); Good, Carter V., ed., *Dictionary of Education* (New York: McGraw Hill, 1973); Isaac, Stephen and William B. Michael, *Handbook in Research and Evaluation* (San Diego: R.R. Knapp, 1971); Leedy, Paul D., *Practical Research; Planning and Design*, 2nd ed. (New York: Macmillan, 1980); Marshall, A.P. ed., "Current Library Use Instruction," *Library Trends* 29 (Summer 1980): 3-172; Millsap, Mary Ann, et al., *Women's Studies Evaluation Handbook* (Washington, D.C.: U.S. Dept. of HEW, National Institute of Education, 1979); and Suchman, Edward, *Evaluative Research; Principles and Practice in Public Service and Social Action Programs* (New York: Russell Sage Foundation, 1967).

AFFECTIVE OBJECTIVE. An objective that is concerned with attitudes or values.

ATTITUDE SCALE. An instrument such as a test or checklist that is designed to obtain a quantitative measurement of attitudes.

BEHAVIORAL OBJECTIVE. An educational objective that is expressed as an actual performance criterion or as a description of measurable behavior.

COGNITIVE OBJECTIVE. An objective that is concerned with knowing, comprehending, or conceptualizing.

CONTENT ANALYSIS. A detailed appraisal of the information contained in any type of communication. The information is classified by the researcher according to a pre-established set of categories such as favorable or unfavorable comments.

CONTROL. The concept of specifying and manipulating the treatment or conditions introduced into an experiment.

CONTROL GROUP. One of two or more groups that is comparable to the experimental group except that it has not been subjected to the conditions introduced into the experimental group.

CONTROL VARIABLE. A variable that needs to be held constant, controlled, or randomized so that its effect is neutralized, cancelled out, or equated for all conditions.

CORRELATION. The process of determining the degree of relationship between two or more variables. If two variables increase or decrease together, the correlation is positive: if one variable increases while the other decreases, the correlation is negative.

DATA. Facts that any particular situation yields to the researcher. Raw data are facts that have not yet been subjected to analysis.

DEPENDENT VARIABLE. In empirical investigation, the factor hypothesized by the researcher to be functions of the independent variable and whose changes or different states are predicted or explained.

DESCRIPTIVE STATISTICS. Statistics used only for describing the sample from which they are derived; specifically not for describing the larger population or group from which the sample is taken.

DISTRIBUTION. In statistics, an array of the instances of a variable arranged according to their value.

EMPIRICAL RESEARCH. Methods of investigation based on experience or observation.

EVALUATION. A judgment of merit sometimes based solely on measurements such as test scores but frequently based on a synthesis of measurements, critical incidents, subjective impressions, and other evidence in the process of carefully appraising the effects of an educational experience.

EVALUATION INSTRUMENT. In an instructional situation, any of the means used to obtain information about the progress of the learner and the effectiveness of the instruction.

EXPERIMENT. A strategy of investigation in which the researcher manipulates one or more factors and measures the effect of the manipulation on other factors. The purpose of an experiment is to test the reasonableness of a hypothesis by determining if the events it predicts actually do occur in a controlled situation.

EXPERIMENTAL GROUP. A group that is systematically subjected to particular conditions in order to discover the effects of those conditions on the group. The experimental group is then compared with a control group.

EXTERNAL VALIDITY. A characteristic of the information yielded in an evaluation and that is applicable to similar situations beyond the one in which it was collected.

FIELD RESEARCH. Attempts to discover the order and regularity underlying the complex of behaviors in natural settings such as classrooms and libraries.

FORMATIVE EVALUATION. The process of collecting and analyzing information about a program from the time it began. Formative evaluation allows the researcher to change and improve a program while it is still in progress.

GOAL. An object, condition, or type of behavior capable of satisfying a need and toward which action is directed; a goal is more general than an objective.

HYPOTHESIS. An educated guess about the solution to a problem or the cause of an event. This is more generally applicable than the null hypothesis used in statistics. Alternatively, a hypothesis is a tentative, declarative statement about the relationship between two or more variables which may be tested empirically.

ILLUMINATIVE EVALUATION. Sometimes called goal-free evaluation, this process focuses on what actually happened or is happening in response to a program. It is a method that de-emphasizes the attaining of initially formulated goals and objectives, preferring to discover unintended or unexpected consequences.

INDEPENDENT VARIABLE. A factor manipulated by the researcher and not dependent on other variables; its impact on the dependent variable is observed during the course of the investigation.

INFERENTIAL STATISTICS. Statistics using small samples from a group to make inferences as to the statistical characteristics of the total group.

INTERNAL VALIDITY. A characteristic of the information yielded in an evaluation that displays a reasonable correspondence to the phenomena it purports to describe or interpret.

INTERVIEW. A research technique involving the questioning of a subject by a researcher in an attempt to obtain accurate responses. Questions presented in an interview should have the same bias-free characteristics as a well-prepared questionnaire.

MEAN. The average derived from among a set of observations, measures, or scores; probably the most frequently used measure of the central tendency of a distribution.

MEASUREMENT. A quantitative description of any phenomenon and one in which the phenomenon has been compared with an appropriate scale; alternatively, the process of obtaining a numerical description of the extent to which any item possesses some characteristic.

MEDIAN. A mathematical calculation that divides a group in half: fifty percent of the items lie below this figure and fifty percent lie above it.

MODE. A mathematical score that occurs most frequently in a group.

NORM. A single value or range of values constituting the usual performance of a given group. In testing, norms give information about the performance of a specified group on a specified test thereby providing a set of criteria which might be used for purposes of comparison.

NULL HYPOTHESIS. The hypothesis that there is no difference between groups or no relationship between variables. Statistical tests are used to accept or reject the null hypothesis; the researcher usually hopes to disprove a null hypothesis.

OBJECTIVE. A limited aim or specific end in view that is anticipated as desirable. The attainment of an objective can be used to monitor the progress of a program or activity toward a more general goal. In bibliographic instruction an objective is often categorized as general, terminal, or enabling.

OBSERVATION. The act of observing conditions as a means of gathering and recording data. An observation is often referred to as an event, location, or a period of time depending on the type of experiment conducted.

PERFORMANCE EVALUATION. An evaluation that measures certain behaviors or the performance of a particular task in a given setting such as a library, as opposed to a test that determines level of knowledge, facility of recall, or similar student trait.

POPULATION. In inferential statistics, a group of individuals or objects (e.g., test scores) that represent all possible cases. Researchers rarely work with entire populations choosing rather to examine samples which are more manageable.

POST-TEST. In experimental designs, a test given to determine the influence of a variable on the experimental group. Results of the post-test are then compared with results of the pretest or with one or more other post-tests.

PRETEST. A test given to determine the skill, aptitude, or achievement of respondents in order to prepare subsequent instruction.

QUESTIONNAIRE. A list of planned, written questions related to a given topic with space provided for answers from a number of respondents. A common data gathering tool in survey studies and in measurements of opinions and attitudes, the questionnaire permits the observation of data beyond the physical reach of the researcher. Questionnaires may also be used to conduct interviews.

RANDOM SAMPLE. A sample chosen so as to guarantee to each item of the group an equal possibility of being selected with the intention that the characteristics of the sample will approximate the characteristics of the entire group or population.

RELIABILITY. The degree to which a measuring device yields consistent responses. For example, a test is reliable over time if it yields similar scores obtained at different times with the same individuals. In a broader sense, reliability is characteristic of stable, consistent, and dependable research methods, instruments, data, or results.

RESEARCH DESIGN. The plan or the framework of a research study; the entire approach to a problem for research. Among other things, a well-prepared research design adopts methods in accordance with the nature of the data that are collected.

SAMPLE. A portion of a group of individuals or objects drawn from the larger group or population. Researchers deal with samples and use statistics to help them decide if the results obtained from the sample can be used to make generalizations about the larger group or population.

SCIENTIFIC METHOD. An investigative approach in which the objective of the inquirer is to achieve precise and reliable knowledge.

SIGNIFICANCE LEVEL. The probability of obtaining a given result by chance. A technique of inferential statistics, the t-test, for example, is used to evaluate the significance of the difference between the means of two groups.

STANDARD DEVIATION. A value intended to help the researcher see a given observation in relation to the mean; one of the more frequently used measures of variability.

SUMMATIVE EVALUATION. An appraisal of the outcome of a program in order to determine its fate.

SURVEY. An investigation of a field or group in order to discover current practices, trends, and/or norms. In a descriptive survey the researcher maintains a record of his or her findings in order to facilitate interpretation at a later time.

T-TEST. A technique of inferential statistics used to evaluate the significance of the difference between the means of two groups.

TEST. A group of questions to which a student is to respond, the purpose being to produce a representation of student traits, or to determine level of knowledge or facility of recall.

TREATMENT. The condition that is applied to or the activity that is used in the experimental group; examples would be programmed instruction, lectures, or other conditions to be observed.

TRIANGULATION. A term indicating that several different methods of data collection are combined in order to produce a comprehensive understanding of the results. This approach is used to overcome the biases and limitations of a single method.

VALIDITY. The extent to which a test or other instrument actually measures what it purports to measure.

VARIABLE. An element, entity, or factor that is being studied in an empirical investigation; thus, it is a trait that may change from one condition or set of circumstances to another and is usually presented in quantitative form such as a measurement; it must have at least two values.

Bibliography

Items in this bibliography were selected for inclusion by the authors who contributed chapters to *Evaluating Bibliographic Instruction: A Handbook*. Entries are divided into two parts. Part I is an annotated list of books, articles, and pamphlets that were helpful in the preparation of individual chapters and that are recommended for further reading. The annotations were written by the contributing authors and edited by the compiler. Part II is a list of basic textbooks on measurement, statistics and computers in educational research.

Part I

Adams, Mignon. "Effects of Evaluation on Teaching Methods." In *Improving Library Instruction: How to Teach and How to Evaluate*. Ed. Carolyn Kirkendall. Library Orientation Series, No. 9. Ann Arbor, Michigan: Pierian Press, 1979, pp. 97-100.

describes the application of various evaluation methods in a particular program of bibliographic instruction

Alkin, Marvin C., and Carol T. Fitz-Gibbon. "Methods and Theories of Evaluating Programs." *Journal of Research and Development in Education*, 8 (1975), 2-15.

a topical, issue-oriented overview of methods, techniques, and problems in the evaluation of educational programs

Association of College and Research Libraries. Bibliographic Instruction Section. Policy and Planning Committee. *Bibliographic Instruction Handbook*. Chicago: American Library Association, 1979.

discusses guidelines for a bibliographic instruction program; treats administrative considerations and provides a model statement of objectives, model timetable, glossary, and pathfinder

Bloom, Benjamin. *Taxonomy of Educational Objectives. Volume I: The Cognitive Domain.* New York: David McKay, 1956.

a standard work especially useful for its examples of how to write test items for higher level objectives

Bruning, James L., and B.L. Kintz. *Computational Handbook of Statistics.* 2nd ed. Glenview, Illinois: Scott, Foresman, 1977.

contains excellent examples for computing statistics with a calculator

Busha, Charles, and Stephen P. Harter. *Research Methods in Librarianship.* New York: Academic Press, 1980.

an essential source for its careful discussions of experimental designs, computer assisted and survey research, historical research, statistical analysis, unobtrusive methods, and proposal writing

Campbell, Donald T., and Julian C. Stanley. "Experimental and Quasi-Experimental Designs for Research on Teaching." In *Handbook of Research on Teaching.* Ed. N.L. Gage. Chicago: Rand McNally, 1963, pp. 171-246.

an authoritative source for research designs in the field of education

Caro, Francis G.,ed. *Readings in Evaluation Research.* 2nd ed. New York: Russell Sage, 1977.

a fine collection of essays, including reprints of Schulberg and Baker's "Program Evaluation Models and the Implementation of Research Findings," Suchman's "Evaluating Educational Programs," and Deutscher's "Toward Avoiding the Goal Trap in Evaluation Research"

Centra, John A. *Determining Faculty Effectiveness.* San Francisco: Jossey-Bass, 1981.

reviews current research on the evaluation of teaching and provides an appendix on commercially available student rating instruments

Conoley, Jane Close, and Harold F. O'Neil, Jr. "A Primer for Developing Test Items." In *Procedures for Instructional Systems Development.* Ed. Harold F. O'Neil, Jr. New York: Academic Press, 1979, pp. 95-127.

guidelines for writing test items, relying on traditional methods (drawn from standard textbooks) as well as on Bormuth's method of item generation

Cook, Kenneth, and C. M. Greco. "The Ugly Duckling Acknowledged: Experimental Designs for Decision-Making Part I." *Journal of Academic Librarianship,* 3 (1977), 23-28; "Part II." 3 (1977), 85-89.

provides a basic introduction to various concepts of experimental design

Cranton, P.A. and L. H. Legge. "Program Evaluation in Higher Education." *Journal of Higher Education,* 49, (1978), 464-471.

a basic introduction to the purpose and use of evaluation

East, Maurice J., et al. *Evaluation Designs for Practitioners. TM Report No. 35.* ERIC ED 099 430

explains and illustrates four experimental designs in natural settings (such as classrooms)

Fjallbrant, Nancy. "User Education Evaluation." In *Directions for the Decade: Library Instruction in the 1980s.* Ed. Carolyn Kirkendall. Library Orientation Series, No. 12. Ann Arbor, Michigan: Pierian Press, 1981, pp. 71-89.

discusses target groups as well as scope, timing, and methods of evaluation

Fjallbrant, Nancy, and Malcolm Stevenson. *User Education in Libraries.* Hamden, Connecticut: Linnet Books, 1978.

a broadly-based treatment of user education in the United Kingdom, United States, and Scandinavia; includes sections on goals and objectives, evaluation, and case studies

Gardner, Don. "Five Evaluation Frameworks." *Journal of Higher Education,* 48 (Sept-Oct 1977), 571-593.

introduces approaches to evaluation used by prominent educators; these are grouped into categories on the basis of the methodologies employed

Gebhard, Patricia. "How to Evaluate Library Instructional Programs." *California Librarian,* 37 (1976), 36-43.

a workshop report that describes the development of model evaluation forms

Helwig, Jane T., and Kathryn Council, eds. *SAS Users Guide.* Raleigh, North Carolina: SAS Institute, 1979.

a highly regarded statistical package for computers that were developed in the late 1960s

Huck, Schuyler W., W. H. Cormier, and W. G. Bounds, Jr. *Reading Statistics and Research*. New York: Harper and Row, 1974.

makes extensive use of case studies and other examples to help explain research designs and statistical analysis

Isaac, Stephen and William B. Michael, eds. *Handbook in Research and Evaluation*. 2nd ed. San Diego: Edits Publishers, 1981.

discusses the planning and evaluation of research studies with special attention to instrumentation and measurement, statistical techniques, data analysis, the setting of objectives, and report writing

King, David N., and John C. Ory. "Effects of Library Instruction on Student Research: A Case Study." *College and Research Libraries*, 40 (1981), 31-36.

examines the effects of user instruction on student library use and on student perceptions of the library

Kirk, Thomas G. "Bibliographic Instruction—A Review of the Research." In *Evaluating Library Use Instruction*. Ed. Richard J. Beeler. Library Orientation Series, No. 4. Ann Arbor, Michigan: Pierian Press, 1975, pp. 1-30.

summarizes user studies and evaluation studies of particular programs, emphasizing the importance of objectives in evaluation; suggests that a program may be evaluated for its content, its processes, or its end products

Knapp, Patricia B. "A Suggested Program of College Instruction in the Use of the Library." *Library Quarterly*, 26 (1956), 224-231.

treats the formulation of objectives in light of curriculum construction and principles of learning

Lubans, John, Jr. "Evaluating Library User Education Programs." In *Educating the Library User*. Ed. John Lubans, Jr. New York: Bowker, 1974, pp. 232-253.

reviews studies that relate library use to academic achievement; reports on a survey of library users and non-users in order to determine the needs for library instruction

Lubans, John, Jr. "Objectives for Library User Instruction in Educational Media." In *Educating the Library User*. Ed. John Lubans, Jr. New York: Bowker, 1974, pp. 211-220.

discusses the establishment of objectives and their integration into the curriculum from elementary through postsecondary education

Mager, Robert F. *Goal Analysis.* Belmont, California: Fearon, 1972.
practical, readable guide to the preparation of statements of goals

Mager, Robert F. *Measuring Instructional Intent: Or Got a Match?* Belmont,
California: Fearon, 1973.
a guide to the analysis of objectives in relation to performance

Mager, Robert F. *Preparing Instructional Objectives.* 2nd ed. Belmont,
California: Fearon, 1975.
a guide to writing objectives that clearly communicate instructional intent

Miller, Harry G., Reed G. Williams, and Thomas M. Haladyna. *Beyond Facts:
Objective Ways to Measure Thinking.* Englewood Cliffs, New Jersey: Educational Technology Publications, 1978.
a useful tool for constructing multiple-choice questions that test knowledge
and abilities rather than merely facility of recall

Millsap, Mary Ann, et al. *Women's Studies Evaluation Handbook.* Washington,
D. C.: National Institute of Education, 1979.
although intended for women's studies directors and faculty, this pamph-
let is useful for academic librarians; it defines evaluation and discusses goals,
objectives, data analysis, and methods of experimental design

Morris, Lynn Lyons, ed. *Program Evaluation Kit.* 8 vols. Beverly Hills,
California: Sage, 1978.
eight handbooks on various aspects of evaluation, designed for practical
use by those who must evaluate programs; titles in the series include:
*Evaluator's Handbook, How to Deal with Goals and Objectives, How to Design
a Program Implementation, How to Measure Achievement, How to Measure
Attitudes,* and *How to Present an Evaluation Report.*

Nie, Norman, and C. Hadlai Hull. *SPSS, Combined Edition.* New York:
McGraw-Hill, 1981.
complete documentation for a computer statistical package that is highly
regarded and widely available

Nielson, Erland Kolding, "Aims and Objectives for User Education." In *NVBR
Anglo-Scandinavian Seminar on Library User Education, Proceedings.* Ed.
Nancy Fjalbrant. Gothenburg, Sweden: ERIC, Nov. 2-4, 1976, pp. 55-59.

Parlett, Malcolm, and David Hamilton. "Evaluation as Illumination." In *Curriculum Evaluation Today: Trends and Implications.* Ed. David Tawney. London: Macmillan, 1976, pp. 84-101.

a critique of the classical "agricultural-botany" approach to evaluation and a proposed alternative approach drawn from social anthropology

Payne, David A., ed. *Curriculum Evaluation: Commentaries on Purpose, Process, and Product.* Lexington, Massachusetts: Heath, 1974.

an excellent collection of essays on the evaluation of education programs; Payne's prologue to the volume, "Toward a Characterization of Curriculum Evaluation," provides a good introduction to evaluation

Person, Roland. "Long-Term Evaluation of Bibliographic Instruction: Lasting Encouragement." *College and Research Libraries,* 40 (1981), 19-25.

examines long-term effects of a bibliographic instruction course on students' achievements and attitudes

Popham, W. James. *Educational Evaluation.* Englewood Cliffs, New Jersey: Prentice-Hall, 1975.

discusses evaluation in the context of program goals and objectives

Provus, Malcolm. *Discrepancy Evaluation for Educational Program Improvement and Assessment.* Berkeley, California: McCutchan, 1971.

discusses how to establish criteria for evaluation

Renford, Beverly, and Linnea Hendrickson. *Bibliographic Instruction: A Handbook.* New York: Neal-Schuman, 1980.

a practical description of how to plan instructional programs; discusses the preparation of handouts, workbooks, and bibliographies

Roid, Gale H., and Thomas M. Haladyna. *A Technology for Test-Item Writing.* New York: Academic Press, 1982.

summarizes new theoretical constructs for test-item writing; not for beginners

Tyler, Robert W., ed. *Perspectives of Curriculum Evaluation.* Chicago: Rand-McNally, 1967.

this collection of articles by expert evaluators includes a revised edition of Michael Scriven's classic, "The Methodology of Evaluation"

University of Texas at Austin. General Libraries. *A Comprehensive Program of User Education for the General Libraries, The University of Texas at Austin.* Austin, Texas: University of Texas, 1977.

identifies the needs and defines the goals and objectives of user education; provides an outline of the program and an appendix of sample materials

Vargas, Julie E. *Writing Worthwhile Behavioral Objectives.* New York, Harper and Row, 1972.

provides instruction in the writing of cognitive objectives; offers a good example of the application of Bloom's *Taxonomy of Educational Objectives*

Vogel, J. Thomas. "A Critical Overview of the Evaluation of Library Instruction." *Drexel Library Quarterly,* 8 (1972), 315-323.

emphasizes the importance of determining the information needs of library users and their perceptions of libraries (and librarians) as a prerequisite to the establishment of instructional objectives

Werking, Richard H. "Evaluating Bibliographic Education: A Review and Critique." *Library Trends,* 29 (1980), 153-172.

a literature review that is essential for its critical analysis of the strengths and weaknesses of the evaluation of bibliographic instruction

Worthen, Blaine R. and James R. Sanders, eds. *Educational Evaluation: Theory and Practice.* Worthington, Ohio: Charles A. Jones, 1973.

includes Robert Stake's influential "The Countenance of Educational Evaluation," Daniel Stufflebeam's introduction to decision-oriented evaluation, "Evaluation as Enlightenment for Decision-Making," and Lee Cronbach's classic, "Course Improvement through Evaluation"

Wotruba, Thomas R., and Penny L. Wright. "How to Develop a Teacher-Rating Instrument." *Journal of Higher Education.* 46, (1975), 653-663.

summaries of twenty-one research studies

Young, Arthur P. "Research on Library User Education: A Review Essay." In *Progress in Educating the Library User.* Ed. John Lubans, Jr. New York: Bowker, 1978, pp. 13-28.

a survey of the research literature from 1972 to 1977 that identifies trends and their implications for future studies

Young, Arthur P. "Research on Library User Education: A Review Essay." In *Educating the Library User.* Ed. John Lubans, Jr. New York: Bowker, 1974, pp. 1-17.

summarizes research that has met at least one of the following criteria: (1) uses statistical inference, experimental design, or intensive case studies, (2) states a hypothesis, or (3) includes multi-institutional surveys

Part II

Backstrom, Charles H. *Survey Research.* Evanston, Illinois: Northwestern University Press, 1963.

Ebel, Robert L. *Essentials of Educational Measurement.* 2nd ed. Englewood Cliffs, New Jersey: Prentice-Hall, 1972.

Fletcher, Leon. *How to Deliver a Speech.* New York: Chandler, 1973.

Gronlund, Norman E. *Measurement and Evaluation in Teaching.* 4th ed. New York: Macmillan, 1981.

Hays, William Lee. *Statistics.* 3d ed. New York: Holt, Rinehart and Winston, 1981.

Lewin, Miriam. *Understanding Psychological Research.* New York: John Wiley and Sons, 1979.

Lien, Arnold J. *Measurement and Evaluation of Learning.* 4th ed. Dubuque, Iowa: W.C. Brown, 1980.

Mehrens, William, and Irving J. Lehman. *Measurement and Evaluation in Education and Psychology.* New York: Holt, 1973.

Oppenheim, Abraham N. *Questionnaire Design and Attitude Measurement.* New York: Basic Books, 1966.

Payne, Stanley R. *The Art of Asking Questions.* Princeton, New Jersey: Princeton University Press, 1951.

Pope, Jeffrey L. *Practical Marketing Research.* New York: AMACOM, 1981.

Runyon, Richard P., and Audrey Haber. *Fundamentals of Behavioral Statistics.* 3d ed. Reading, Massachusetts: Addison-Wesley, 1976.

Selltiz, Claire, Laurence S. Wrightsman, and Stuart W. Cook. *Research Methods in Social Relations.* 3d ed. New York: Holt, Rinehart and Winston, 1976.

Shaw, Marvin, and Jack M. Wright. *Scales for the Measurement of Attitudes.* New York: McGraw-Hill, 1967.

Spatz, Chris, and James O. Johnston. *Basic Statistics: Tales of Distributions.* 2nd ed. Monterey, California: Brooks/Cole, 1981.

Weinberg, George H., and John A. Schumaker. *Statistics: An Intuitive Approach.* 3d ed. Monterey, California: Brooks/Cole, 1974.

Welkowitz, Joan, Robert B. Ewen, and Jacob Cohen. *Introductory Statistics for the Behavioral Sciences.* 3d ed. New York: Academic Press, 1982.

John Mark Tucker
Purdue University

Index

119